## AUTHOR

**Eduardo Manuel Gil Martínez** (25 June 1970) is a historian and has been passionate about Spanish history for several years, mainly about the Second World War and the age of the Reconquista. Author of numerous texts on the Second World War for Spanish and Italian magazines such as 'Revista Española de Historia Militar', AMARTE, 'Ritterkreuz' or 'The Axis Forces in the Second World War 1939-1945'. In addition to the title we publish, he is also the author of: "Sevilla Reina y Mora. Historia del reino independiente sevillano. Siglo XI', 'Breslau 1945. El último bastión del Reich', 'The Spaniards in the SS and the Wehrmacht. 1944-45. The Ezquerra unit in the Battle of Berlin ",' The Bulgarian Air Force in World War II. The forgotten ally of Germany', 'Romanian Armoured Forces in the Second World War', 'Hungarian Armoured Forces in the Second World War', 'Spanish Air Force in the Second World War', 'Hispano Aviación Ha-1112' (about the last Messerschmitt 109 ever built in Spain) and other texts for important publishers such as Almena, Kagero, Schiffer and Pen & Sword.

For the photos, we would like to thank:
FORTEPAN: Berkó Pál, Tarbay Julia, Doboczi Zsolt, Kókány Jenő, Ludovika, Varga Csaba dr., Csorba Dániel, Lissák Tivadar, Nagy Gyula, Konok Tamas Id, Miklós Lajos, Gadoros Lajos, Lakatos Maria, Marics Zoltán, Nagypal Geza, Vargha Zsuzsa, Lázár György, Mihalyi Balazs, Klenner Aladar, Scrutatore Ferenc, Kramer Istvan Dr, Ungvary Krisztian, Károly Németh, Péter Mujzer.

## PUBLISHING'S NOTES

None of unpublished images or text of our book may be reproduced in any format without the expressed written permission of Luca Cristini Editore (already Soldiershop.com) when not indicate as marked with license creative commons 3.0 or 4.0. Luca Cristini Editore has made every reasonable effort to locate, contact and acknowledge rights holders and to correctly apply terms and conditions to Content.
Every effort has been made to trace the copyright of all the photographs. If there are unintentional omissions, please contact the publisher in writing at: info@soldiershop.com, who will correct all subsequent editions.
Our trademark: Luca Cristini Editore©, and the names of our series & brand: Soldiershop, Witness to war, Museum book, Bookmoon, Soldiers&Weapons, Battlefield, War in colour, Historical Biographies, Darwin's view, Fabula, Altrastoria, Italia Storica Ebook, Witness To History, Soldiers, Weapons & Uniforms, Storia etc. are herein © by Luca Cristini Editore.

## LICENSES COMMONS

This book may utilize part of material marked with license creative commons 3.0 or 4.0 (CC BY 4.0), (CC BY-ND 4.0), (CC BY-SA 4.0) or (CC0 1.0). We give appropriate attribution credit and indicate if change were made in the acknowledgments field. Our WTW books series utilize only fonts licensed under the SIL Open Font License or other free use license.

For a complete list of Soldiershop titles please contact Luca Cristini Editore on our website: www.soldiershop.com or www.cristinieditore.com. E-mail: info@soldiershop.com

Title: **HUNGARIAN ARMOURED UNITS DURING THE SECOND WORLD WAR - VOL. 1: 1938 - 1943**
Code.: **WTW-047 EN** by Eduardo Manuel Gil Martínez
ISBN code: 9791255890355 first edition October 2023
Size: 177,8x254mm. Cover & Art Design: Luca S. Cristini

**WITNESS TO WAR (SOLDIERSHOP)** is a mark of Luca Cristini Editore, via Orio, 33/D - 24050 Zanica (BG) ITALY.

**WITNESS TO WAR**

# HUNGARIAN ARMOURED UNITS DURING THE SECOND WORLD WAR

## VOL. 1: 1938 - 1943

PHOTOS & IMAGES FROM WORLD WARTIME ARCHIVES

**EDUARDO MANUEL GIL MARTÍNEZ**

BOOKS TO COLLECT

# CONTENTS

**PREFACE**......................................................................................................................5

**THE BIRTH OF THE HUNGARIAN ARMOURED FORCES**..................................7
   THE NECESSARY MAGYAR REARMAMENT..............................................................7

**1938: HUNGARY TRIES TO MAKE ITS WAY IN EUROPE**..................................11
   FIRST COMBAT ACTIONS........................................................................................11

**1939: WORLD WAR II BEGINS**..............................................................................13
   THE DICE START ROLLING.....................................................................................13

**1940-1941: HUNGARY COMES UNDER THE GERMAN 'UMBRELLA'**.............15
   THE PACT WITH GERMANY....................................................................................15
   THE 1941 USSR CAMPAIGN....................................................................................16

**1942: ACTIONS IN UKRAINE**................................................................................39
   OCCUPATION TASKS AND RETURN TO THE FRONT LINE..............................39
   FIRST BATTLE OF URYV..........................................................................................49
   FIRST BATTLE OF KOROTOYAK............................................................................51
   SECOND BATTLE OF URYV.....................................................................................56
   SECOND BATTLE OF KOROTOYAK.......................................................................58
   THIRD BATTLE OF URYV.........................................................................................59

**1943: DISASTER AND REORGANISATION**.........................................................73
   THE SOVIET ROLLER MAKES ITS APPEARANCE...............................................73
   ARMOURED FORMATIONS IN THE OCCUPATION TROOPS.............................90
   DISENGAGE FROM GERMANY, BUT HOW?........................................................91

**ANNEX: INSIGNIA OF THE HUNGARIAN ARMOURED FORCES**....................93

BIBLIOGRAPHY............................................................................................................98

# PREFACE

The performance of the German armoured forces during the Second World War is well known. However, less well known is the performance of the armoured forces of Germany's allies. Although they were generally rather minor, if not disappointing, the performance of the Hungarian armoured forces must be emphasised. In recent times, authors such as Péter Mujzer and Czaba Becze have explored this aspect in depth, shedding light on a subject largely unknown even to fans of the history of the Second World War and the Axis in particular. Another work of great interest, covering more general aspects of the Hungarian role in World War II, is that of Bernád y Climent, although not yet published in full.

Despite Hungary's obvious industrial limitations after being 'dismembered' in the aftermath of the First World War, the country was able to develop the necessary infrastructure for the domestic production of tanks and other armoured vehicles. Although these units were not up to the standards of the German ones, they were welcome in the Axis military effort, which generally relied on German industrial potential. Hungary's initial self-sufficiency in armour production meant that the overburdened German arms production did not have to worry too much about the Hungarian ally, at least for the first two-thirds of the war. Later, it had to supply armoured fighting vehicles in larger quantities due to the desperate Hungarian military capabilities after the numerous setbacks suffered in the battles against the all-powerful USSR.

Another noteworthy aspect of Hungary's wartime history is that it remained on the side of Germany until the end of the conflict, despite various attempts by the Hungarian government to break the alliance. One way or another, this meant that Hungary became a recipient of German equipment until the last months of the fighting in Europe, including some of the best German tanks such as the Tiger and Panther. The reluctance of the Germans to allow the arrival of their most modern and powerful weapons to any other country is well known, but the Hungarian ally earned the Germans' recognition for its behaviour in combat.

In this text, we will explore Hungarian participation during the Second World War, beginning with the invasion of the USSR and continuing with involvement in the battles along the Eastern Front, up to the battles on the Hungarian plateau and the final conflicts on Austrian and Slovenian territory before the unconditional surrender.

It is well known that central European cities often had names based on the country that controlled them. In the case of Hungary and its historical territories, we find that the same city can be recognised by three or four different names. In general, and because of the topic we are dealing with, we have preferred to use the name given by the Hungarians to these cities, followed in brackets by the name given to them today. Thus, for example, we will use the name Temesvár (Timisoara) to refer to that city, since this is the name by which the Magyars called it.

Although this text will deal with the Hungarian armoured forces, we will often also deal with other military groupings, both Soviet and German, in order to provide a more general view of the fighting than we would have if we limited ourselves to them alone. Given the simultaneous battles along the Hungarian front, especially in 1944 and 1945, we have chosen to separate them into the various most significant campaigns or battles to facilitate understanding.

In all the situations in which the Hungarians had to fight, often under difficult conditions, they did so with great courage and daring despite the enemy's superiority in terms of men and modern weapons. This text is a tribute and a remembrance of those men involved in a conflict whose consequences influenced the history of the country for the next 45 years.

▲ The obsolete Hungarian FIAT 3000B tank (the famous Renault FT-17 tank was the model on which the FIAT 3000 was based), was completely technologically outdated when the Second World War began. The production process began in May 1919.

# THE BIRTH OF THE HUNGARIAN ARMOURED FORCES

## THE NECESSARY MAGYAR REARMAMENT

The history of the Hungarian armoured forces during the Second World War (WWII) was marked by the secondary role that Germany relegated its European allies to. Advances in military technology during the conflict years were so rapid that the industries of countries such as Hungary, Romania and Italy were never able to keep up with the level of development and, of course, the amount of production achieved by the Soviets and the United States. This led to a heavy reliance on German industry for support, but the circumstances of the war prevented this support from being sufficient for these satellite countries to catch up with their Soviet rival.

Despite considerable limitations, Hungarian industry managed to build an indigenous armoured force, to which various types of vehicles of Czech or German origin were added, eventually making Hungary the Germans' most reliable ally in terms of armaments.

▲ A Hungarian soldier proudly poses next to a camouflaged Ansaldo tank of Italian origin.

But to understand the evolution of these armoured forces, we must go back to the end of the First World War, when, subject to the conditions of the Treaty of Versailles of 1919, the Austro-Hungarian Empire was dismembered into several countries, and Austrian territory mutilated in several areas by the Treaty of Trianon of 1920. With the former, the Hungarian armed forces were radically limited in the quantity and quality of their equipment; with the latter, Hungary lost part of Transylvania (which passed to Romania), Rijeka, Slovakia, Croatia, Vojvodina and Bosnia-Herzegovina, resulting in the loss of important natural resources and a large part of its population, which was integrated into other countries. The objective was clear: to prevent the country from taking up arms again.

The Treaty of Trianon was a great economic bankruptcy for the country, as the loss of territory was compounded by the loss of human material and, of course, natural resources. As a result, Hungarian industry was almost wiped out, but what little remained was of great importance in the years to come. We are referring to the Manfred Weiss engine company and the MAVAG locomotive company, which in the years of the Second World War would become the foundations of the national military industry, which would eventually be far superior to that of other neighbouring countries.

The Hungarian army under the regency of Admiral Miklós Horthy was thus limited to 35,000 men in seven mixed brigades without armour. Infantry units remained at the pre-GWP level, with virtually no machine guns, mortars (only 70 light and medium mortars) or heavy artillery (only 105 10.5 cm howitzers). Of course, the new kings of the battlefield, such as aircraft and armoured vehicles, were completely banned.

The situation was very difficult for Hungary, but it became even more so when in the 1930s all her neighbours managed to rearm to a much greater extent than she did. Czechoslovakia, Romania and Yugoslavia became far superior in terms of arms and numbers and, as if that were not enough, signed mutual assistance treaties, leaving Hungary partially surrounded and defenceless.

Faced with everything that could come its way (Czechoslovakia had the country's few industrial areas a stone's throw away), the Hungarian Army tried to ensure that its small numbers would not be a limitation for adequate preparation to make it an effective fighting force capable of stopping any invasion attempts by its neighbours. But this was not enough, so in 1934 an external ally was sought, which was none other than the emerging Germany. In the same year, 1934, Hungary began to increase its war potential by acquiring foreign material, in particular 150 Italian CV-33 Fiat-Ansaldo tanks (as these vehicles were obsolete, most of them remained in storage and only 15 were used for training purposes) and 12 Fiat L2 armoured vehicles.

It was at this point that the figure of Nicholas Strausser emerged, a Hungarian who had lived for years in the UK and who, on his return, designed a wheeled armoured vehicle based on the Alvis C2, which he named Csaba. It was armed with a 20 mm cannon, which, together with its mobility, allowed Honved to quickly order 100 units, which were produced by Manfred Weiss.

Strausser himself designed a prototype tank, but it was rejected by the Hungarian government, so licences for the production of another model had to be sought abroad. The Swedish Landswerk L-60 tank was chosen, of which it was decided to build 80 units in Hungary. It was given the name Toldi I. Although it was a tank, it lacked a cannon and armour suitable for the time, as its 20-mm cannon and 13-mm frontal armour thickness were by no means up to the standard of tanks of the time. It is true that attempts were made to compensate for this lack of armour by increasing it to 35 mm in the next order of another 80 Toldi, in this case called Toldi II.

When Nazi Germany began to exert more influence in Europe, Hungary became wary and tried to find new solutions. The result was the Bled Agreement of 1938 between Hungary and its rival neighbours to relax some of the restrictions of the Treaty of Trianon, which included not only non-aggression against Hungary, but also the possibility of creating an air force and increasing the size and composition of the army.

Hitler, with his Germany in the midst of a rearmament process, did not accept this agreement willingly, so the export of war material to Hungary was very limited. Once again, Hungary found itself under the crossfire of its powerful neighbours. One section of Hungarian public opinion looked favourably on Germany, especially after the 1938 Anschluss on Austria and the Sudetenland (belonging to the Czechoslovak enemy). Another important group of opinion preferred rapprochement with Mussolini's Italy, another rising power in Europe.

▲ The Hungarian FIAT 3000B tanks did not participate in the armed conflict due to obsolescence, although in this photo, taken in 1942, they were still in service.

▲ Only one prototype of the Straussler V4 of Hungarian origin was produced, which was not followed up.

# 1938: HUNGARY TRIES TO MAKE ITS WAY IN EUROPE

## FIRST COMBAT ACTIONS

In 1938, following Germany's territorial claims on Czechoslovakia, Hungary seized the opportunity to recover part of its territories lost during the First World War. Although these claims put both the Hungarians and Czechoslovaks in full combat readiness, eventually, on 5-10 November of the same year, the historically Hungarian northern territories were peacefully occupied by four infantry corps with a total of seven tank companies.

The long-awaited break-up of Czechoslovakia was exploited by Hungary to assert, now by force, its rights over Ruthenia (part of the territory that had been Hungarian and was now part of Czechoslovakia). In this case, the German Reich was also opposed to Hungarian intentions but, based on the fact that the Hungarian population in Ruthenia was large, decided to go ahead.

The campaign began on 15 March 1939 with the advance of the VIII Mobile Corps; the first skirmishes took place at Francsika (Francikovo) and Nagyszöllös (Novy Sel) at dawn on the same day. The Hungarian onslaught against the enemy troops was so rapid that on the 17$^{th}$ the Hungarian Ansaldo tank companies reached the Polish border. During their advance, war materials were captured from the opponents, including a fully intact Lt. 35 (or Pz 35). Attacks by Slovak Letov S.328 aircraft against the 2$^{nd}$ Motorised Artillery Battalion were recorded until 24 March.

After a short resistance by Czech, Slovak and Ukrainian nationalist troops, the Hungarians reached their objectives in less than ten days: the eastern part of Ruthenia, Ungvar and Münacks, which were thus annexed.

With regard to the combat performance of armoured vehicles, it was clear that most Ansaldo tanks could not withstand an engagement against an underpowered enemy for less than two weeks. Mechanical problems, breakdowns and lack of spare equipment completely decimated these Italian armoured vehicles.

However, Hungary, after its lightning-fast action, was once again gaining a certain weight in the militarised Europe of the late 1930s; but it was only a deceptive image that time would soon unmask.

205
2F

▲ These Ansaldo tanks of the 2nd Reconnaissance Battalion somewhere in Transylvania in 1940 show why the national emblem was not much appreciated by the crews. They were a real moving target.

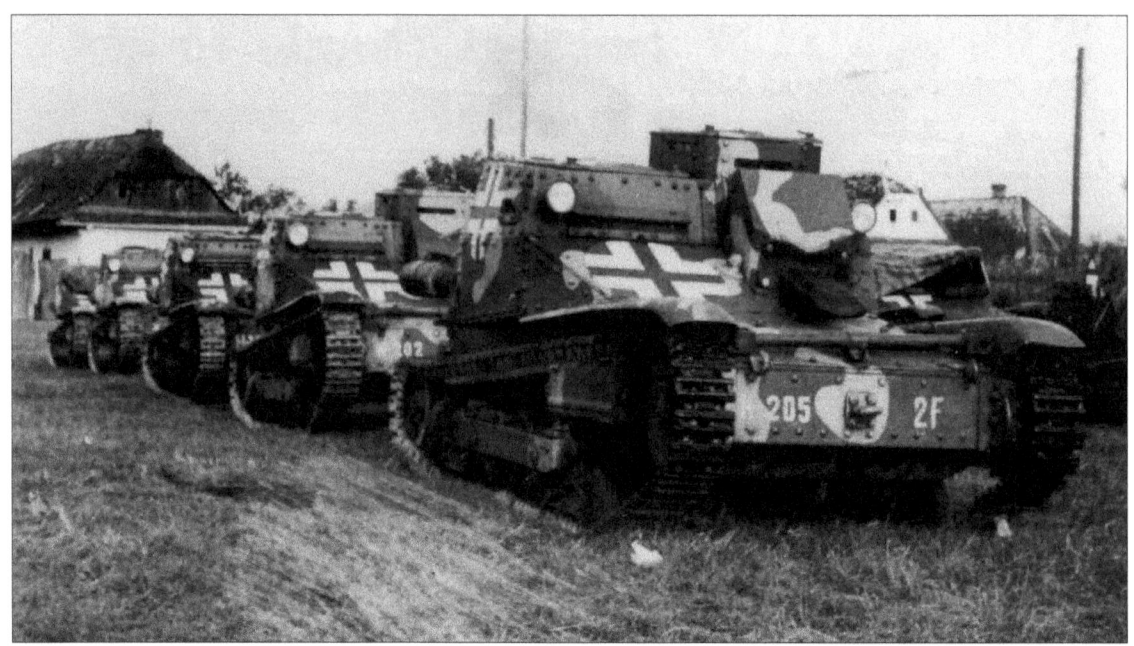

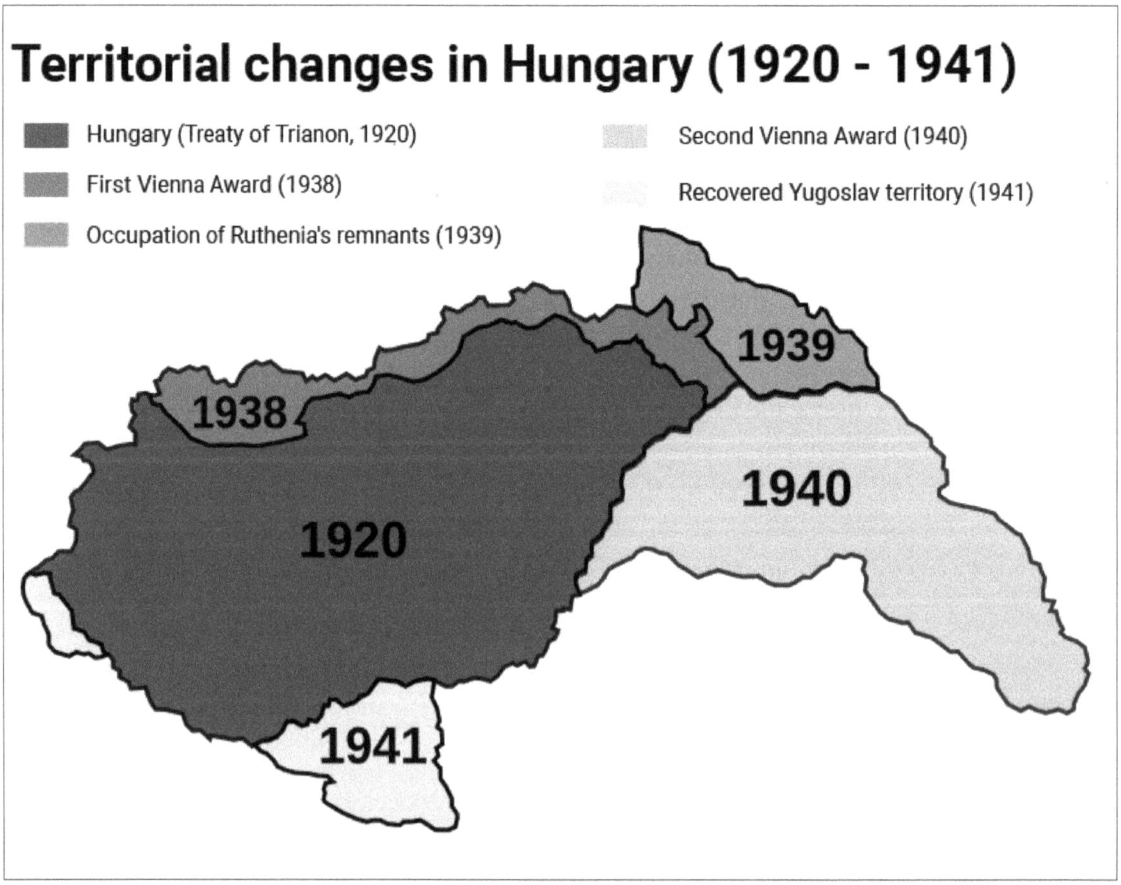
Territorial changes in Hungary (1920 - 1941)
Hungary (Treaty of Trianon, 1920)
First Vienna Award (1938)
Occupation of Ruthenia's remnants (1939)
Second Vienna Award (1940)
Recovered Yugoslav territory (1941)
1939
1938
1940
1920
1941

# 1939: WORLD WAR II BEGINS

## THE DICE START ROLLING

Only a few months after the capture of Ruthenia, the Second World War began. At that point, the Hungarian army consisted of 9 army corps, 1 mobile corps, 25 divisions and 18 regiments, as well as other mixed border units, etc. Of these, the Mobile Corps, which was the flagship of the army and included two motorised brigades and two cavalry brigades, as well as other smaller units, deserves special attention.

The outbreak of world war brought a new movement to Hungary, which finally saw the time to free itself from the restrictions imposed by the Treaty of Trianon. Its army began to grow at a dizzying pace, despite the ban, because it had been undergoing military training since the end of World War II and only needed to be restructured. It was now more necessary than ever to acquire better and more modern war material, both from the limited domestic industry and from abroad. Germany and Italy were of course the main suppliers, both of their own material and that from the spoils of war of the countries that were being conquered. In fact, after the German attack on Poland, 19 retreating Polish tanks arrived in Hungary and were interned.

In addition to other weapons and concentrating on the appearance of the armoured forces, the T-38 or Pz 38 tanks (from Germany, but of Czechoslovak origin) and the aforementioned Toldi or Csaba (domestically produced) were acquired.

▲ The arrival of some small Polish armoured vehicles in 1939, at the time of the invasion of Poland, slightly increased the Hungarian armoured potential. The photo shows one of the TKS tanks transported on a truck and some Polish soldiers.

▲ Front view of a Toldi I with 20 mm cannon, clearly insufficient for a tank.

# 1940-1941: HUNGARY COMES UNDER THE GERMAN "UMBRELLA"

## THE PACT WITH GERMANY

The new target of belligerent Hungary this time was Transylvania, in the possession of Romania after the Treaty of Trianon. In the summer of 1940, the territory was claimed by the Romanian government (which at the time was threatened by the USSR's claim to the regions of Bukovina and Bessarabia), while the Hungarian army was stationed on the Romanian border in south-eastern Hungary. On this occasion, the armoured troops consisted of the obsolete Ansaldo, the much more valuable 38 M Toldi (40 in total) and the M39 Csaba tank (13 in total), which had recently been incorporated into the Hungarian army and was the pride of the national war industry.

On 28 August 1940, after Romania's claim to Germany as arbiter of the conflict was accepted by the Magyars, the restitution of Transylvania to Hungary was finally confirmed. The actual takeover of the territory by the Hungarians took place between 5 and 13 November. The conclusions of the campaign were very positive from a political point of view, but as far as their armoured forces were concerned, it was the same as the capture of Ruthenia, as the Ansaldo, the Toldi and the Csaba needed urgent maintenance work just for the sake of conquering the wilds of Transylvania and despite the fact that they did not have to fight.

With Germany and Italy around, Hungary finally joined the Axis Tripartite Pact between Germany, Italy and Japan in November 1940.

As the invasion of Poland was followed by confrontation in Western Europe, Hungary continued its process of modernisation and growth without any threat from outside its borders. This period of peace, only partially interrupted by the Transylvania affair, came to an abrupt end when in the spring of 1941 Hungary, as a consequence of its membership of the Axis, participated in the German invasion of Yugoslavia, supporting its ally. Germany did not really need Hungarian military support, but with the promise of being able to annex the (previously Hungarian) Drava territory, it agreed to do so.

The mode of participation was through the Hungarian 3rd Army, which began its advance on 11 April in the direction of the Danube near Baranya (only five days earlier the bulk of the German troops had begun the attack on Yugoslavia). The Hungarian 3rd Army consisted of the I, IV and V Corps and the Mobile Corps. With regard to the latter, one could see the gradual addition of the new 38M Toldi and 39M Csaba to the already heavily battered 35M Ansaldo. Nevertheless, the Hungarian troops were not fully equipped and manned.

The Hungarian troops met slight resistance from the Yugoslav 1st Army, which could be crushed without much effort after limited fighting at Topolya (Backa Topola) on the 11th, Szettamás (Srbobran) on the 12th and 13th, Petröc (Backi Petrovac), Dunágalos (Glozan) and Újvidék (Novi Sad) on the 13th.

The number of casualties in the Yugoslav campaign was rather low due to the weak resistance of the Magyars, so that the great limitations of the Hungarian armoured forces and the

▲ A Csaba tank passes a checkpoint controlled by Hungarians at the front.

Hungarian armed forces in general were not yet evident.

## THE 1941 USSR CAMPAIGN

Only with Operation Barbarossa, launched on 22 June 1941 against the Soviet Union, did Hungary face an enemy that would make life very difficult for it. Hungary did not initially participate in this operation, but after the alleged Soviet bombing of the Hungarian towns of Kassa and Munkacs on 26 June, war was declared against the USSR on 27 June. The bombing actually caused little material and human damage, but the reaction of the Hungarian army and press, which demanded revenge for such a cowardly act, led to war on the eastern front. It is unclear whether the bombing was Soviet or not, but it is certain that it served to make Hungary join the German war effort.

On 27 June 1941, the Hungarian troops of the so-called Carpathian Group, consisting of the Mobile Corps (known as Gyorshadtest), the 1st Mountain Brigade and the 8th Frontier Brigade, began to advance with an estimated strength of 44444 men towards Soviet territory from the Carpathian front under the command of Lieutenant General Ferenc Szombathelyi, being integrated into the German XVII Army. The 8th Frontier Brigade had the task of conquering and controlling the Uszok Pass in the Carpathians to secure access to the easternmost part of Hungary. Gyorshadtest was assigned to the Huzst-Marmarossziget-Borkut area. For the campaign that was being prepared on the Soviet front, the Mobile Corps under the command of Major General Béla dálnoki Miklós was at 75-80% of its optimum potential, but reached a total of 81 Toldi I 38M, 60 Ansaldo 35M and 48 Csaba 39M tanks (later 14 Toldi, 5 Ansaldo and 9 Csaba tanks would be added to replace decommissioned vehicles).

The Gyorshadtest, although the mechanised unit of the EH, was still far from being fully mechanised and its vehicles were already technologically backward compared to what it had to face in the vast Soviet lands. This corps consisted of several units totalling some 25,000 well-equipped men and officers. Its very configuration allowed it to act as an inde-

▲ Signs indicating return to Hungary from Transylvania (Erdély in Hungarian).

pendent unit and, although on paper it was very powerful, in reality it was comparable to a Soviet Motorised Corps.

The immediate deployment of their troops to the USSR was considered of vital importance at the highest Hungarian levels, so these units could not be fully trained, leaving Gyorshadtest, as already mentioned, with only 75-80% of what it should have been, lacking properly trained trucks and horses; although at least in terms of morale and discipline they were ready for combat. Bearing in mind that the time elapsed from the mobilisation of the Mobile Corps until it was considered ready to be sent to the front was only three days.

The composition of the Mobile Corps as at 29 June 1941 was as follows:

- 1ª Motorised Brigade (commanded by Major General Jenö Major).
    - 1st Motorised Battalion.
    - 2nd Motorised Battalion.
    - 3rd Motorised Battalion.
    - 9th Bicycle Battalion.
    - 10th Bicycle Battalion.
    - 1st Armoured Reconnaissance Battalion.
    - 1st Motorised Artillery Battalion.
- 2ª Motorised Brigade (commanded by Major General János Vörös).
    - 4th Motorised Battalion.
    - 5th Motorised Battalion.

- 6th Motorised Battalion.
- 11th Bicycle Battalion.
- 12th Bicycle Battalion.
- 2nd Armoured Reconnaissance Battalion.
- 2nd Motorised Artillery Battalion.

- 1st Cavalry Brigade (commanded by Major General Antal Vattay).
  - 3rd Cavalry Regiment.
  - 4th Cavalry Regiment.
  - 13th Cyclist Battalion.
  - 14th Cyclist Battalion.
  - 3rd Armoured Reconnaissance Battalion.
  - 1st Horse Artillery Battalion.
  - 3rd Motorised Artillery Battalion.

- For the occasion, several units were attached to the Mobile Corps.
  - I, V and VIII Artillery Battalion.
  - Cyclist Battalions VI and VII.
  - 150th Signal Battalion and 152nd Engineer Battalion.
  -

Each of the two motorised brigades that were part of the Mobile Corps had 36 38M Toldi I and 16 39M Csaba reconnaissance vehicles, while the 1st Cavalry Brigade, which had recon-

▲ The long-awaited break-up of Czechoslovakia was exploited by Hungary to assert, now by force, its rights over Ruthenia. During its advance, war material was captured from the adversaries, in particular a completely intact Lt. 35 (or Pz 35), as can be seen in the photo. 35 (or Pz 35) completely intact, as can be seen in the photograph.

▲ The Csaba tank, a flagship of the domestic armaments industry, had very attractive lines, but lacked adequate armour.

▼ Troops of the 13th Cyclist Battalion deploy to the Romanian-Hungarian border in September 1940.

▲ A small column of Ansaldo tanks takes a break. In the centre of the photo a radio operator using an R-3 model radio with a circular antenna.

▼ In the Hungarian advance through Transylvania, the Toldi and Csaba tanks played an important role in their reconnaissance and observation tasks.

naissance missions, was only equipped with 9 38M Toldi I and 36 35MAnsaldo tanks. In general, all this armoured equipment would have had little to do against Soviet anti-tanks. After the conquest of the Carpathian mountain passes at Pantyr and Tatár with the 1st Mountain Brigade, it would be the Gyorshadtest that would bear the brunt of the advance through the Galician region to advance into Ukrainian territory, but this would only be possible after these mountain passes were well secured. The advance was carried out with the intention of repelling and attacking the Soviet 12th Army, consisting of two Rifle Corps (the 13th and 17th) and a Mechanised Corps (the 16th), totalling about 56,000 men along a front line of over 250 kilometres.

The advance started very slowly, due to the numerous mines the Soviets had placed in the mountain passes, the 21 blown bridges, the difficult terrain and the very basic infrastructure of the existing road network. In addition, the Soviets demonstrated a good degree of military preparedness in terms of ambushes and counterattacks aimed at slowing down the Hungarian advance. Due to all these factors, it was only possible to penetrate into enemy territory for about ten kilometres during the first four days, after the conquest of the town of Tatarov in the foothills of the Carpathians. The Magyars' use of their armoured units left much to be desired, as they were not used in the right way or at the right time, perhaps due to a lack of experience in their use in real combat.

It was only when the mountain passes were left behind that Gyorshadtest began to show its true potential to penetrate the vastness of the USSR.

The attack on the 12th[a] Army began at dawn on 1 July and, despite numerical inferiority and heavy losses, the Hungarians managed to first repel and then push back the Soviets, making an advance into enemy territory of about 100 kilometres. By 7 July, the Dniester had been

▲ Two Csaba tanks awaiting their new mission in 1940. Although poorly armoured, they were used extensively by the Hungarian armoured reconnaissance forces.

crossed and a bridgehead had been created on its easternmost bank. Due to the high speed of this advance, the 1st Mountain Brigade and the 8th Frontier Brigade, which were marching on foot, were unable to follow the Gyorshadtest. Given the inability of these brigades to follow the mobile corps, Colonel General Werth (Chief of the Hungarian General Staff) disbanded the Carpathian Group, deploying these units to guard the occupied territory and leaving the Gyorshadtest at the disposal of Marshal von Rundstedt's German Army Group South.

Already following other German units, the Gyorshadtest took part in several battles, acting decisively in some of them, even if at the cost of suffering a significant number of losses, both human and material. Facing them were the Soviets who, although in continual retreat, continued to sell every kilometre advanced in their territory at a high price.

As part of the German 17th Army, the Gyorshadtest participated in the march towards Kiev. On 10 July, they captured the towns of Kamenets-Podolskiy and Smotrich. Later, the Gyorshadtest was assigned to the German 1st Panzer Group, which made it the main rival of the Soviet 17th Rifle Corps for several weeks.

The deplorable condition of the roads caused the commander of the Mobile Corps on 11 July to opt to replace the motorised troops stuck in the mud with cavalry troops as the spearhead of his unit. This enabled further progress, capturing Zwanczyk and Kurilova on 13 July and Rogosnec (near the Bug River) on 19 July. In the fighting between 19 and 22 July (aimed at capturing the Stalin Line), the Hungarians destroyed numerous Soviet vehicles and captured at least 13 tanks and 12 artillery pieces, breaking the Soviet defensive line. In the Petschara area alone, they destroyed at least 21 tanks, 16 armoured vehicles and 12

▲ Another Csaba tanker taken out of service by an enemy mine in Vojvodina in April 1941. From the tarpaulin covering it, this one should have been sent to a repair service in the rear to try to put it back into service.

artillery pieces. Losses were not long in coming and at least 6 38M Toldi I were destroyed and 7 damaged, leaving 3 39M Csaba out of action. On the 23rd, a Hungarian attack by the 2ª motorised brigade in Kopiyevka succeeded in dismantling the Soviet positions. Only two days later, the towns of Trostianczyk and Gordiyevka were captured.

Analysing these numbers, it might appear that the Hungarian armoured vehicles were a tough nut to crack for the Soviets, and although in a sense they were at this time, this was due to the fact that they faced Soviet armoured forces also consisting of obsolete armoured vehicle models such as the BT-2 the BT-5, the BT-7, the T-26, the T-37 and the T-38 which, although they had larger calibre guns than their Magyar opponents, still lacked adequate armour to withstand the 20mm guns of the Toldi I 38M.

Within a couple of weeks, the Hungarian armoured units had received a major setback from the Soviets, but also one of no less significance due to the harshness of the contested terrain. With so many vehicles out of service, civilian workers from the Manfred Weiss, Ganz and MAVAG factories were sent to the front on 18 July to put as many vehicles as possible (including at least 30 Ansaldo tanks) back into service.

Between 22 and 29 July, during the combing of the Soviet troops still positioned west of the Bug River, heavy fighting (especially in the Budy area) led to the loss of 32 Toldi and 18 Ansaldo tanks (the Soviets, however, only lost two tanks in action). Resistance was increasingly fierce and the losses began to create serious doubts about the forthcoming clashes

▲ Part of the Hungarian vehicle fleet were motorbikes with sidecars, which provided speed and versatility, as well as a place for crews to rest. Here an officer tries to sleep on his CWS M111 Sokol 1000.

▲ Csaba Company of the 2nd Armoured Cavalry Battalion in Vojvodina in April 1941.

▼ Hungarian parade led by Ansaldo tanks in September 1940 in a village in Transylvania.

▲ A Csaba tanker temporarily out of service after falling into a snowy ditch.

with the Soviets. The Ansaldo once again proved unreliable in rough terrain and under heavy stress: on many occasions, the engine would stop in action. The only way to start it was from the outside with a crank, which was an easy target for the poor crewmen who had to do it. This action marked the beginning of the end of the use of these tanks at the front for obvious reasons.

To make matters worse, the Hungarian advance coincided geographically with that of their Romanian 'ally', so the Germans acted quickly to allow the Gyorshadtest to continue its advance into the Ukraine without contacting them. Nevertheless, on 28 July, in the only instance where they were on their flank, the 3rd Calarasi Regiment of the 8th Romanian Cavalry Brigade retreated in the face of the first Soviet attack they received, consequently leaving the Hungarian right flank in danger. To avoid further damage, the gap on the right flank was filled by the Hungarians themselves, who eventually managed to take the village of Versad, near Gordiyevka, during the fighting.

To compensate for the high number of losses of the armoured units, 14 38M Toldi I, 9 39M Csaba and 5 35M Ansaldo were sent from Hungary by rail on 27 July. They arrived at their destination on 7 October, so we can imagine how chaotic communication with the front was. On 31 July, the Gyorshadtest was south-west of Umán, west of the Bug River, assisting German troops in encircling important Soviet units (the Soviet 6th and 12th Armies) in that area. The next day, the Hungarians with their armoured spearhead succeeded in crossing the Bug River at Gayvoron, managing to take Pervomaisk on the 2nd, where they linked up with the German 16th Panzer Division. From that dazzling offensive, the Magyars set about halting their advance and attempting to hold the newly occupied territories, where numerous Soviet troops (the 6th and 12th Armies) had been left behind their lines in what was to be called the Uman pocket. Thus, in collaboration with the German troops, they reinforced a second encirclement line around these Soviet units (the first ring consisted of German troops) by controlling several bridges to prevent any Soviet attacks from outside aimed at liberating their compatriots. In this defensive configuration, Hungarian troops were left to the south and west of the pocket.

But, contrary to what one might think, the danger did not come from outside the pocket, but from within it. On the 6th, a pair of Csaba on a reconnaissance mission under the command of what was to become Second Lieutenant László Merész spotted a Soviet cavalry group studying the weak points of the encirclement; they drove them back with fire from their vehicles. But the pressure from inside the pocket grew so great that the encircled Soviet troops launched a heavy attack with the intention of breaking through the encirclement

▲ Picture of a row of four Ansaldo 35M tanks in an occupied village in the Carpathian area showing troop movements.

▲ Poorly armed and poorly armoured Ansaldo 35M tanks, marching through the streets of a city towards the front, could do little in combat.

▼ The Toldi I performed adequately in muddy terrain, but its lack of armour was a handicap to its overall design.

▲ The Gyorshadtest, part of the German 17th Army, participated in the march towards Kiev. On 10 July 1941, they captured the towns of Kamenets-Podolskiy and Smotrich. The photo shows a T-26 and a couple of destroyed trucks between Kamenets-Podolskiy and Tulcsin. This T-26 was seen in the foreground in an earlier photograph.

in two directions (the 6th Army to the south and the 12th Army to the east), which they succeeded in doing by breaking through the first line of defence where the German 257th Division was deployed on 6 August. However, the Soviets were unaware of the existence of the second ring of encirclement, which caused them to persist in trying to escape to the positions held by the Hungarians, which they attacked but ultimately failed to overcome. The troops that had to fight the Soviets were the 1st Cavalry Brigade, which was already on the alert after hearing the sounds of Soviet fighting against the men of the 257th Division. Major General Vattay quickly sent in support the men of the 3rd Armoured Battalion, who cut off the breakaway attempt to the south, closing the pocket again. The 2nd Hungarian Motorised Brigade also moved from its positions at Dzulinka and attacked the encirclement from the west. Meanwhile, the reconstituted German troops attacked from the east with the 100th and 101st Light Divisions. Thanks to the brilliant Hungarian action, the encircled Soviets (about 100,000 men) finally surrendered on 8 August, which allowed the Axis troops to make important advances on the western bank of the Dnieper in the subsequent counter-offensive, controlling several crossing points of the Dnieper.

Further south, the advances of the German and Romanian troops were reaching their objectives, so an attempt was made to pocket several Soviet armies, including the 9th and 18th between the Bug and Dnieper rivers. From the 8th itself, the Gyorshadtest was integrated into the 1st Panzer Group and took part in this operation from the eastern bank of the Bug River. Together with a company of Italian riflemen, the Hungarians of the 1st Motorised Bri-

▲ One of the virtues of the Ansaldo tank was its speed, which reached 43 km/h in favourable terrain. A group of these tanks from the 1st Armoured Cavalry Battalion advancing towards the front posing for the camera in March 1939 during the occupation of the Carpathians.

▼ Troops on bicycles struggle through a village to reach their destination.

gade blocked the bridges over the Bug River between Pervomaisk and Konstantinovka. The Brigade was then sent south between the Bug River and the Nikolayev-Vozsiyatske highway, with the rest of the Gyorshadtest following shortly afterwards. The advance did not prove to be easy, as they were heavily attacked from the air, so much so that during the 10th and 11th two light tanks and 12 armoured vehicles were lost, and 10 trucks were damaged.... Immediately the Hungarians received orders to take Nikolayev along the course of the Bug River, for which they were supported by their own air force in the form of Ju-86K bombers and CR.42 and Re-2000 fighters. The long distances covered and the shortage of petrol for the Hungarian vehicles caused a delay in the advance and the consequent improvement of Soviet defensive positions; the Hungarian offensive towards Nikolayev had to be considered a failure as it did not achieve its objectives. The German 16th Panzer Division was immediately assigned to achieve this objective and the Hungarian troops were subordinated to the Germans.

Continuing the advance, the Hungarians of the 1st Motorised Brigade captured the village of Sukhoy Yelanets between 10 and 11 August. Between 12 and 14 August, several battles took place near Novaya Odessa, until the town was finally captured by the Germans and the Hungarians managed to hold back the enemy to allow the Germans to advance.

The Gyorshadtest then continued the advance, with the 1st Motorised Brigade taking the

▲ The Hungarian field artillery was already obsolete at the outbreak of hostilities, a problem that generally persisted until the end of hostilities.

▼ Hungarian motorised troops wait their turn to cross a river. On the bridge, the ubiquitous Hungarian-made Botond truck.

▲ A Raba Botond off-road vehicle towing a trailer. Image taken in 1941.

▼ Ceremony of the 15th Cyclist Battalion where an Ansaldo tank can be seen, as well as other anti-tank and machine guns.

▲ Several damaged armoured vehicles assembled in a Honvéd barracks in Mátyásföld. One can see a Csaba tank on the left, a Soviet BT-7 tank in the centre of the photo and a Turán tank on the right.

▲ Csaba tank destroyed in July 1941 in Rogazna (USSR). Its poor armour did not make it very resistant to enemy fire, although it was not of large calibre.

- Hungary during World War II -

  ○  Hungary in 1920

  ∞  Hungary in 1941

  —  Borders within Axis-controlled Europe (as of 1941)

▲ The Toldi light tank, although inferior to its Soviet enemies, was of great use to Hungarian armoured troops on reconnaissance missions.

▲ Several Toldi tanks were developed and shortly afterwards sent to their combat units. This Hungarian-made tank was named 38M Toldi in honour of the 14th century Hungarian warrior Miklos Toldi.

▼ Magnificent image of a Turan I armed with its 40 mm cannon. Poorly armoured and poorly armed, it was never up to the standard of rivals such as the T-34 or the KV-1.

▲ Close-up of some Csaba tanks that served so well during the conflict. The vehicle on the left is still awaiting armament.

towns of Ingulka and Peresadovka on the 15th. Meanwhile, the 2nd Motorised Brigade carried out "combing" work in the southern and south-eastern parts of Novaya Odessa; and the 1st Cavalry Brigade took part in the encirclement around Nikolayev. The assault on the latter on 16 August involved all units of the Gyorshadtest, with a Hungarian cavalry charge supported by machine guns, a pair of anti-tank guns and perhaps 4 or 5 39M Csaba from the 1st Cavalry Brigade's Armoured Reconnaissance Battalion covering the flanks. Nikolayev was taken on the 17th, but not before a large number of Soviets had managed to escape the encirclement.

The Mobile Corps was immediately instructed to take up position on the right bank of the Dnieper River for about 200 km to the left of the Romanian 3rd Army. For a few days (17 to 27 August), it was able to enjoy a well-deserved rest period. Initially, the Hungarian troops, which were not very large, managed to cover such a vast area with great effort, but on 5 November, a major Soviet attack on the defensive line of the 2nd Motorised Brigade near Zaporozhets forced them to retreat with heavy losses in terms of men and equipment. This retreat provoked the Magyar rearrangement, which led to the withdrawal of the 1st Motorised Brigade from its positions (its place was taken by German troops) from positions near Nikopol. This move reduced the dispersion of the Magyar units to 150 km, a more reasonable distance considering the poor fighting conditions at Gyorshadtest.

It was during this deployment on the banks of the Dnieper that the Hungarian leadership, led by Horthy, began to doubt whether its troops would remain at the front. The first step towards their repatriation was the dismissal of the pro-German Werth, who was replaced on 5 September 1941 by Colonel General Ferenc Szombathelyi. From the beginning, Szombathelyi was convinced that his army should only be used for the defence of the country's borders, but he quickly clashed with the German allies. His approach was that the best Hungarian units should be on Hungarian territory to prevent any attack from Romania (the rivalry between the two countries was intact even though they had fought in the USSR on the same side and even shoulder to shoulder in some cases), especially in the Transylvania region. To force the Germans to accept this new strategy, he prevented any maintenance or replacement of vehicles lost during the Gyorshadtest campaign. Between 8 and 9 September, the Führer's headquarters decided on the partial repatriation of the Hungarians on the eastern front: the 1st Cavalry Brigade could return to Hungary immediately, but the remaining units (the Mobile Corps, the 1st Mountain Brigade and the 8th Frontier Brigade) would only return when Hungary provided four Infantry Brigades for occupation and second-line duties on the Soviet front. The German decision to return was due to the very low combat value and the urgent need to reorganise the Hungarian troops, which did not prevent the weakened Hungarian Mobile Corps from continuing to be used until 24 November of the same year. However, between 27 September and 11 October, the Mobile Corps was granted a break from combat actions in order to reorganise and recover its combat strength as much as possible.

Throughout their stay at the front, the Magyars showed great courage and a sense of duty that led them to several victories against a more plentiful and better equipped Soviet enemy. And although always subordinate to German orders, on at least one occasion they managed to act independently (after Dalnoki-Miklos refused the orders of his superior officer

Runstedt). It was on 19 October when, after the Battle of Kiev, the depleted Gyorshadtest was ordered to frontally attack the Soviet defences that had previously repelled a multitude of German attacks. The Hungarian force numbered six battalions and disaster was on the horizon, so Dalnoki-Miklos opted for a manoeuvre to encircle the Russian troops, allowing the advancing German advance into the USSR to keep the road to Voroshilovgrad open. On 28 October, the Hungarian troops managed to reach their objective, the town of Isium on the Donets River.

The Mobile Corps was withdrawn from action on the front line and on 6 November the repatriation to Hungary finally began.

The result of just under five months of heavy fighting, with the difficulty of maintaining their vehicles, combined with the lack of replacement for the fallen, was the cause of the overall disastrous results: around 200 officers and 2500 men were killed, 1500 were missing in action and around 7500 were wounded. The armoured equipment was decimated, with the loss of all Ansaldo tanks, 80% of the Toldi I medium tanks and 90% of the remaining armoured vehicles. On the other hand, the Hungarian troops had captured over 8,000 Soviets and 65 guns, managing to destroy about 50 tanks. In addition, the Hungarians had advanced over 1,000 kilometres into Soviet territory, participating in the Uman sack, the capture of Nikolayev, the occupation of the Dnieper bank, reaching the Donets, etc. Despite this, the Germans' opinion of the Hungarians was generally positive, although the lack of adequate military equipment, including antiquated armoured forces, severely limited them. After the experience on Soviet soil, the Hungarian High Command realised that further expansion and improvement of the army and its armoured forces was necessary. This planning was called 'HUBA Plan II', which was a continuation of the HUBA Plan I that had taken place before the Second World War. These changes were noticeable from late 1941 onwards, but it was in 1942 that the plan was finally completed.

Although off-topic, during the rest of 1941, it is worth mentioning the action of the Hungarian occupation units stationed on the eastern front, in the town of Reumentarovka. There, on 21 December, a Hungarian light division succeeded in eliminating the active partisan group under General Orlenko, which was continuously striking at the rear of the Axis advance. In this action, the Soviets suffered at least a thousand casualties, including dead, wounded and captured.

# 1942: ACTIONS IN UKRAINE

## OCCUPATION TASKS AND RETURN TO THE FRONT LINE

At the beginning of 1942, Hungarian participation on the Eastern Front was limited to the aforementioned occupation units operating in the rear.

But the active participation of the Hungarians at the front was far from over, because in planning operations for the summer of 1942, Germany demanded maximum Hungarian assistance in the fighting on the Eastern Front. In fact, Germany's initial request was for almost the entire Hungarian army. Against this, and after arduous negotiations, the Hungarians offered their 2nd Army as an alternative. Hitler accepted this option and ordered the subordination of the Hungarian 2nd Army to one of his Army Groups.

This new Magyar unit, with about 200.000 men, was assembled under the command of Colonel General Gusztav Jany and consisted of three army corps (III Corps with the 6th, 7th and 9th infantry divisions, IV Corps with the 10th, 12th and 13th infantry divisions and VII Corps with the 19th, 20th and 23rd infantry divisions), the 1st Armoured Division and several independent units such as the 51st Battalion and the 51st Armoured Battalion, (the 12th and 13th Infantry Divisions and the VII Corps with the 19th, 20th and 23rd Infantry Divisions), the 1st Armoured Division and several independent units such as the 51st Anti-Aircraft Self-propelled Battalion, the 1st Reconnaissance Battalion, the Signal Battalion, etc.

▲ A Turan I advances into a combat zone. On the side of the road, Magyar troops can be seen pausing.

▲ The prototype Toldi I performs an exercise to demonstrate its cross-country capabilities. Despite the great leap forward of the Hungarian military industry, it was a tank far below what was required in Europe at the start of the Second World War.

▼ A pair of Pz 38s passes through a village during the advance into Soviet territory. Although it represented an important step for the Magyar armoured forces, it was already obsolete when it was purchased by the Germans.

▲ Hungarian soldiers observe a Soviet T-28 tank taken out of service in 1942.

At least on this occasion, the Hungarian armoured forces had improved compared to 1941, mainly due to the acquisition of equipment from the German arsenals, such as the Panzer 38 (also Pz 38 or Skoda 38 (t)) or the Panzer I and IV F-1 (perhaps there were also some D models), together with the national Toldi light tanks (the Turán were not yet available, so the burden of the unit fell on vehicles from Germany). The 1$^{st}$ Armoured Division, due to the recent arrival of new equipment, and the entire 2$^{nd}$ Army in general, suffered from a lack of units in its various constituent units.

In order to make the best use of the new German vehicles, specific training was organised for future vehicle crews. Thus, between 10 January and 17 March, 38 officers, 120 soldiers and 52 mechanical technicians were trained in Wunsdorf (Germany). On their return to Hungary, they were sent to Esztergomtábor, where the Armoured Division was already being organised.

Once training was completed and ready to be sent to the front, the 1$^{st}$ Armoured Division had 12500 men, 185 armoured vehicles, 453 motorbikes, 1491 trucks, 325 cars and 106 other miscellaneous vehicles. The unit was also equipped with 24 37 and 50 mm anti-tank guns, 22 105 mm howitzers, 8 80 mm anti-aircraft guns, as well as mortars, anti-tank guns and heavy and light machine guns.

Within the 1$^{st}$ Armoured Division, its flagship was the 30$^{th}$ Armoured Regiment, consisting of two battalions. Each battalion had one heavy tank company with 11 Pz IV F-1, 3 Pz 38 and 1 38M Toldi; and two medium tank companies with 20 Pz 38 each. In addition to all the aforementioned vehicles, there were the 3 Pz 38 and two 38M Toldi modified as medical vehicles of the battalion staff; the 3 Pz 38, 2 38M Toldi and 6 command vehicles of the regimental staff; the 6 Pz 38 of the reserve tank platoon and 2 38M Toldi.

▲ Miklos Horthy inspects the interior of a Pz IV F1. One notices the Hungarian emblem of the time, consisting of a green cross with white borders on a red octagon.

▼ Impressive demonstration of Magyar battleship strength with numerous Pz 38 and Nimród ready for action.

All this brings us to a total number, at the level of the 30th Armoured Regiment, of 104 Pz 38, 22 Pz IV F-1, 6 Toldi and 6 Pz I; which allows us to appreciate how the Hungarian-made Toldi practically disappeared from combat units, and that the 35M tanks did so completely, being recycled for surveillance tasks in the interior of the country.

In addition to the 30th Armoured Regiment, other armoured vehicles were present in the 2nd Army: the 40-metre Nimrod armoured anti-aircraft vehicle and the 39-metre Csaba tank.

The Hungarian-built 40M Nimrod anti-aircraft armoured vehicle was part of the 51st Anti-Aircraft Self-propelled Battalion, which had three companies with 6 40M Nimrods and 1 38M Toldi I commanding each company. To these should be added 3 38M Toldi and 1 40M Nimrod from Battalion Headquarters.

The 39M Csaba was an integral part of the 1st Reconnaissance Battalion, whose armoured vehicle company consisted of 14 units.

For its part, the signal battalion had 4 38M Toldi I

Finally, the Depot Division consisted of a Replacement Company with four Pz 38 and two Pz IV F-1.

▲ A brand new Toldi shows the coat of arms of the Maltese Cross on the front and side of the turret in 1941. The emblem of the Hungarian mechanised troops is also visible on the turret.

▲ Although Hungarian armoured troops performed well in combat, they always lacked an adequate number of modern tanks to match their Soviet enemies. The photograph shows a Pz IV F1 in the foreground with the Hungarian plate on the front.

▼ Nimród anti-aircraft vehicles demonstrating the lifting power of their cannon during manoeuvres. Only 135 of these magnificent vehicles were produced in Hungary, but they played an important role in the battles in which they participated.

▲ The Nimród adequately fulfilled its anti-aircraft and anti-tank mission despite the 40 mm calibre of its gun, thanks to its high rate of fire.

▼ A column of reconnaissance Csaba tanks pauses briefly before continuing the march.

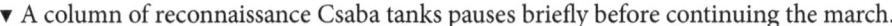

The order to march into German-controlled Ukraine did not take long to arrive, although, due to logistical impossibilities, it had to be executed in three consecutive stages. The first to leave on 11 April were the 2$^{nd}$ Army Headquarters and the 3$^{rd}$ Army Corps (with the 6$^{th}$, 7$^{th}$ and 9$^{th}$ Light Divisions), followed on 30 May by a second contingent of the 4$^{th}$ Army Corps (with the 10$^{th}$, 12$^{th}$ and 13$^{th}$ Light Divisions) and finally by the 7$^{th}$ Army Corps (with the 19$^{th}$, 20$^{th}$ and 23$^{rd}$ Light Divisions), the 1$^{st}$ Armoured Division and the rest of the 2$^{nd}$ Army personnel. To move the 2$^{nd}$ Army to the Eastern Front, 875 trains with an average of 55 freight cars each were required.

Part of General Jany's Hungarian 2$^{nd}$ Army (especially the 3$^{rd}$ Army Corps, with the rest of the army components lagging behind) was attached to Marshal von Bock's Army Group B, which also consisted of the 4$^{th}$ Panzer Army, the German 2$^{nd}$ and 6$^{th}$ Armies and the Romanian 3$^{rd}$ Army; its mission was to support the left wing of the German advance towards Stalingrad. This Army Group, together with Army Group A, was to be the protagonist of the Blue Case (the German plan of operations for the summer of 1942 on the southern part of the Eastern Front). On Hitler's orders they were integrated into the German machine between the 6$^{th}$ and 2$^{nd}$ Armies (with the exception of the 6$^{th}$ Light Division, which was left about 300 km west of Kursk with anti-partisan rearguard missions). As the Germans supported the bulk of the frontline attack, the troops from the Allied countries (Hungarians, Italians and Romanians) would remain as reserve troops to cover the Don front.

The first movements that would lead to the city of Stalingrad were carried out by the Weichs Army Group (reporting to Marshal von Hoth), which comprised the 4$^{th}$ Panzer Army, the German 2$^{nd}$ Army and the 3$^{rd}$ Army Corps of the Hungarian 2$^{nd}$ Army (at the time consisting only of the 7$^{th}$ and 9$^{th}$ Light Divisions, so the Germans supported them with the 387$^{th}$ Infantry Division and the 16$^{th}$ Motorised Division). The advance would take place from the Kursk region towards Voronczh, with the Hungarians covering the right flank of the German advance. Facing stiff Soviet resistance, the Hungarians of the 9$^{th}$ Light Division were chosen on 28 June 1942 to take the town of Tim, reaching it two days later and finally capturing it on 2 July.

Subsequently, the regrouped Hungarian 2$^{nd}$ Army (including the 1$^{st}$ Armoured Division) was ordered to control a sector of the banks of the Don River, arriving in its deployment area on 7 July. The Hungarian 2$^{nd}$ Army was to be positioned along a 200-kilometre stretch of the western bank of the Don River with the main objective of defending it and thus preventing any Soviet attack attempts. At this time, the Soviets still had three bridgeheads in the western sector of the river: at Uryv, Korotyak and Shchuche (Shchuchye), which were very dangerous because they were in direct contact with the Hungarian positions. These three were to be the main targets assigned to the Magyar troops, although the bridgeheads at Uryv and Korotyak would stand out, while the one at Shchuche was so small that neither the Hungarians nor the Germans were concerned. In order to have their armoured forces available in any area of their surveillance zone, they were deployed in the second line as they were considered the reserve of the 2$^{nd}$ Army.

The order of battle of the 1$^{st}$ Armoured Division at that time was as follows (according to Stenge and Cloutier):

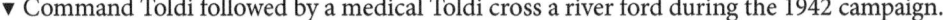

▲ A column of Pz IV F1s from the Heavy Tank Company of the Hungarian Tank Battalion advances into Soviet territory during the 1942 campaign.

▼ Command Toldi followed by a medical Toldi cross a river ford during the 1942 campaign.

- 30th Armoured Regiment.
    - 30/I Armoured Battalion (with Companies 30/1, 30/2 and 30/3).
    - 30/II Armoured Battalion (with Companies 30/4, 30/5 and 30/6).
- 1st Motorised Rifle Brigade.
    - 1st Motorised Rifle Battalion.
    - 2nd Motorised Rifle Battalion.
    - 3rd Motorised Rifle Battalion.
- 51st anti-aircraft self-propelled battalion.
- 1st Motorised Signal Battalion.
- 1st Medium Motorised Howitzer Battalion.
- 5th Medium Motorised Howitzer Battalion.
- 2nd Anti-Aircraft Battalion.
- 1st Reconnaissance Battalion.
- 1st Engineer Company.
- 1st Traffic Control Company.
- 1st Motorised Supply Battalion.

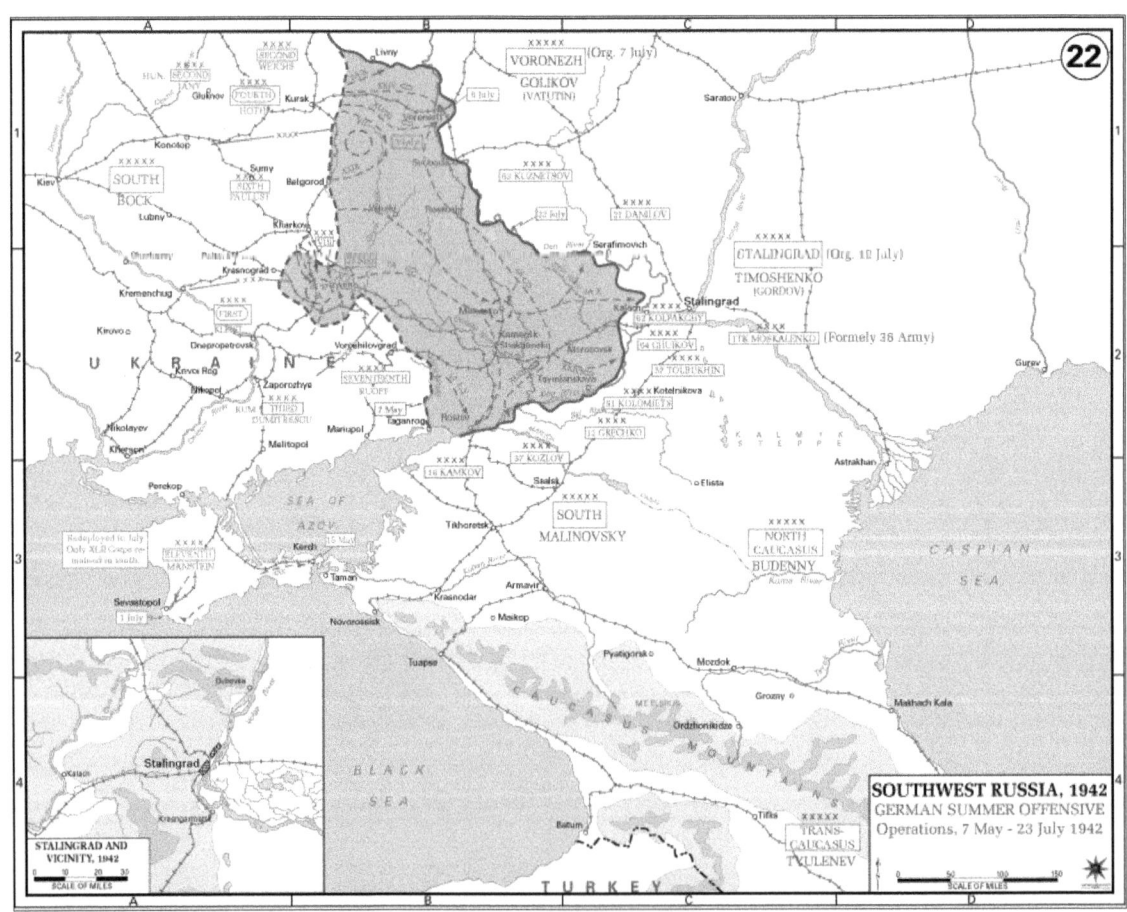

▲ Axis offensive in the Soviet Union between 7 May and 23 July 1942. Public domain.

Starting on 8 August, the Soviets attacked the Hungarian town of Kosteni. After several advances and counter-moves, the attackers were repulsed, although not completely, as they remained to occupy a small strip of marshy land on the west bank of the Don.

Colonel General Jány, commander of the 2nd Army, seeing the great danger to his troops in light of what had happened at Kosteni, considered it imperative to take action against the Soviet bridgeheads, so he prepared his troops, in particular the 1st Armoured Division, for this purpose. His first target: Uryv.

## FIRST BATTLE OF URYV

On 18 July, the 7th Light Division, supported by the 1st Armoured Division, broke off hostilities. For the occasion, a battle group was created (as the Germans did on numerous occasions during the conflict) consisting of the 30th Armoured Battalion, the 51st Anti-Aircraft Self-propelled Battalion and the 1st Motorised Rifle Battalion. Alongside these, other units, mainly cavalry and artillery, provided support.

It was the 30/3 Tank Company, under the command of Captain Makláry, that struck the first blow against the Soviet troops of the Soviet 24th Armoured Corps (which had over 100 tanks, including the mighty T-34/76, as well as T-60s, KV-1s and M3 Stuarts). In this attack, the Hungarians managed to knock out 21 enemy armoured vehicles, more than half of which were PZ IVs, which were already beginning to give the Hungarian armoured force some power (in this engagement, Corporal Roszik with his Pz IV managed to destroy four enemy tanks). The Hungarians' opponent was the Soviet 130th Armoured Brigade (the other two units of the 24th Armoured Corps, the 4th and 54th Armoured Brigades, had been withdrawn in the face of the Hungarian attack), which, despite its T-34/76 and M3 Stuart, was completely eliminated from the bridgehead after heavy losses. In this engagement, the 40M Nimrod anti-aircraft vehicles proved that their usefulness could also extend to ground combat. In fact, as the 30/1 Company advanced, the Nimrods of the 3rd Company of the 51st Anti-Aircraft Self-propelled Battalion (commanded by Captain Henkey-Hönig) supported

▲ BMW R-75 and Puch 350G sidecar motorbikes belonging to the 3rd Motorcycle Company.

it. Suddenly, the tanks of the Soviet 130th Armoured Brigade swooped in from behind and flanked the Pz 38s. The Nimrods aimed their 40mm guns at the Soviets and at a distance of 500-600 metres launched their volleys of fire, knowing how futile the effort could be. Luck favoured the Hungarian anti-aircraft, however, as one of the shots managed to pierce the pilot's view of a T-34 and destroy it. The same fate befell five other tanks (in this case M3 Stuarts of American origin) in the face of continuous Nimrod fire. The Hungarians then continued their advance and managed to inflict another heavy blow on the Soviets, who were deployed on top of some hills overlooking the river, which at the time was the escape route for many Red Army men, using a multitude of small boats of various types. Many of these were destroyed by fire from the Pz IVs and Nimrods, as well as a couple of tanks that appeared on the eastern bank of the river. In return, at least one Pz IV was damaged by the enemy, although it was later recovered.

During the fighting, the Hungarian troops received air support from their own aircraft. In particular, four Ca.135 4/1 bombers were responsible for dropping up to four tons of bombs on the entrenched enemy.

After the first day of fighting, the Hungarians had succeeded in eliminating the Soviets from the bridgehead, destroying at least 31 Soviet tanks and capturing four (possibly all of the Stuarts). However, the Soviet counter-offensive was not long in coming and that very night, coinciding with the lack of German supplies to the Hungarians to support the attack, the Hungarians managed to retake their positions at Uryv, pushing back the Hungarians who were finally withdrawn to their original positions on 20 July.

Of the four captured Stuarts, three were used as tugs in the same Armoured Division, while the fourth was sent to Hungary for study and testing.

▲ Several Turán II tanks stored under cover in a military depot awaiting shipment to their destination unit.

This combat against the Soviets made it clear that the only weapon that could guarantee success against the powerful Soviet armour was the 75-mm cannon of the Pz IV, as the 37-mm cannons of the Pz 38 or the 40-mm cannons of the Nimrod could only cause damage to the enemy at very short distances and only if they were the older models of the Soviet armoured arsenal. From the point of view of the readiness of the Hungarian armoured forces, it was clear how well they utilised the training received from the German instructors. It was they who taught the tactic of waiting for the T-34 crews to be blinded by smoke from their own guns so that they could attack them from more advantageous positions in a wraparound manoeuvre.

## FIRST BATTLE OF KOROTOYAK

Immediately after the end of the Battle of Uryv, and due to the continuous build-up of Soviet forces in the bridgeheads on the Don, the Hungarian General Staff decided to attack again, but in this case the position chosen would be the village of Korotoyak, where the enemy had increased in numbers in the last few hours. The 10th Light Division had been forced back by the 73rd Rifle Regiment and the 174th Rifle Division. Once again the bulk of the attack would be carried by the 1st Armoured Division, reinforced by the depleted 12th Light Division (which had just arrived after a six-week march to the front) and supported from the air by Ca.135s, which would drop some 7 tons of bombs on the Soviets. The Hungarians managed to deploy 103 PZ 38s, 20 PZ IVs, 12 40M Nimrods, 7 38M Toldi, as well as seven anti-tank guns. This battle would become known as the First Battle of Korotoyak.

▲ Maintenance workshop where some Turán tanks were overhauled in 1942.

▲ A column of 40M Nimród in 1944. Although equipped with a 40 mm cannon with a high rate of fire at a cadence of 120 rounds per minute was no match for Soviet tanks, this fast armoured vehicle more than proved its power against enemy light vehicles, infantry or cavalry.

7 August at 6am was the date and time chosen for the armoured troops' advance towards the Don, with the aim of eliminating the Soviet troops stationed there. Despite the successful advance of the Hungarian armoured troops from the west of the city, the enemy's resistance was so stubborn that they did not flee from their positions (also thanks to the support of 12 T-34s supporting them from the other side of the river). The cost of the first day of battle was three Pz 38s destroyed along with five others of the same model and two Pz IVs temporarily out of action. The Soviets lost over 400 men killed and captured and lost at least one light tank that was captured.

The next day, an attack by more than 20 Soviet tanks was repelled and four of them were destroyed. Later the Hungarian tanks were used as assault artillery to eliminate areas of Soviet resistance, partially succeeding on 9 August. This success also had its downside in the form of losses for the 1st Armoured Division, which lost 38 Pz 38, 2 Pz IV and 2 38M Toldi, as well as 387 casualties. It is true, however, that the repair services on the second line managed to bring some of these tanks into service.

Following this success, the men of the 1st Armoured Division were urgently recalled to Uryv to support the 7th Light Division.

▲ BT 7 captured by the Soviets and put on public display in 1942.

▲ T-26 knocked out by the Magyars.

▲ A Hungarian Pz 38 destroyed after the fighting. The licence plate of the vehicle is clearly visible.

## SECOND BATTLE OF URYV

As already mentioned, the Uryv bridgehead after the first battle was reinforced by the Soviets. Among the Soviet units, one of the newcomers was the 116th Armoured Brigade with a large contingent of T-34s, T-60s and T-70s.

On 10 August, the Hungarians, led by the 1st Armoured Division and the 13th Light Division, began a new attack, which proved unsuccessful. The heavy Soviet anti-tank firepower destroyed the 30th/1st Armoured Battalion 10 Pz 38; heavy losses were also inflicted on the infantry troops. The result was first a halt to the advance and shortly afterwards a retreat to the starting line of the Hungarian counterattack.

▲ KV-1 put out of action by the Hungarians in 1942.

▲ Several Nimród in column prepare to fire towards the roadside.

## SECOND BATTLE OF KOROTOYAK

It did not take long for a new Soviet attack to hit the Hungarians again. On 8 and 9 August (the dates do not completely coincide according to existing sources), a new offensive from the Korotoyak bridgehead clashed with the pre-announced Hungarian defences. The attack was led by the 174th Rifle Division, which had been crossing the Don since 8 August to take up positions before the offensive, conducted without artillery preparation to surprise the defenders.

The Hungarians resisted the first blow at the cost of losing considerable areas of ground, but the attack continued the following day with increased losses among the defenders. The transfer of units of the 1st Armoured Division on the 9th to the Uryv bridgehead (second battle), which left only the 30/II Armoured Battalion at Korotoyak, also did not help and the Soviets took advantage of this to increase their attacks. Despite this, the tanks of the 30/II managed to hold off the attackers.

▲ French tanks, such as this cleverly camouflaged Somua S-35, were used by second-line units in anti-partisan tasks, due to their obsolescence for front-line fire. This photo shows a tank of the 101st Independent Tank Squadron in a Polish village in mid-1943.

After the end of the Battle of Uryv, the 1st Armoured Division returned to the vicinity of Korotoyak, which allowed for a counter-attack on 15 August in which the 12th Hungarian Light Division and the 687th German Infantry Regiment, among others, participated. On this day, at least 10 Soviet tanks (T-60s and M3s) were destroyed, while on 30/3, a Pz IV was lost to a mine (which, under the command of its commander Hegedüs, had previously destroyed four M3s). Three Pz 38s from 30/I Battalion were also lost, although curiously, two of them were lost to 'friendly' fire from the 687th Regiment. The T-34s proved their superiority over the 'underdog' Pz 38s, whose losses increased by a further three units the following day, after having to withstand a new Soviet thrust joined by the 957th Rifle Regiment supported by T-34s.

The attrition suffered by both sides was so great that the intensity of the fighting diminished in the following days, until the front line stabilised again around 18 August, after the Hungarians and Germans had been driven out of Korotoyak and the surrounding area.

Hungarian losses were heavy and mainly involved the 1st Motorised Rifle Brigade and the 1st Reconnaissance Battalion, of which 15 Pz 38 were captured by the Soviets. After the Second Battle of Korotoyak, only 55 Pz 38 and 15 Pz IV remained in service.

After this fighting, the Hungarians were finally withdrawn from Korotoyak and their positions were occupied by the German 336th Infantry Division, which succeeded in capturing the bridgehead in early September. This had further repercussions, as the Soviets decided to concentrate their forces on the Uryv bridgehead from then on.

The Hungarians had managed to hold their own against the Soviets, but the cost in terms of human lives and especially armoured equipment led the Germans to decide to reinforce the 1st Armoured Division with four Pz IV F2s (which were an improvement over the Pz IV F1s held by the Hungarians, as they were equipped with 75 mm L/43 long guns instead of 75 mm L/24 short guns). These tanks were received at the end of August and significantly increased the fighting capability of the Hungarians.

We must not forget the performance of the 51st Anti-Aircraft Self-propelled Battalion in these battles, which shot down between 38 and 40 enemy aircraft (out of a total of 63 shot down by the various units that made up the 1st Armoured Division).

## THIRD BATTLE OF URYV

By the beginning of September, the 1st Armoured Division, thanks to reinforcements from the Germans and the repair and recommissioning of some tanks lost during previous fighting, had increased its numbers to 85 Pz 38, 22 Pz IV (F1 and F2) and 5 38M Toldi. Above all, it had increased the number of Pz IVs, which remained the only reliable opponents in combat against the growing T-34s.

He was soon back in action as General von Lagermann's XXIV German Armoured Corps prepared for a new attack on the Uryv bridgehead, scheduled for 9 September, with the intention of destroying it once and for all.

The disposition of the attackers was as follows: on the left flank were the 168th German Infantry Division and the 20th Hungarian Light Division supported by the 201st Assault Cannon Battalion with Stotozhevoye as the target; and the 13th Hungarian Light Division on the right flank with Uryv as the target, while the 1st Armoured Division supported the entire front line with its armoured vehicles. The Hungarian 7th and 12th Light Divisions would also take part in the fighting.

The left wing attack met strong resistance in the vicinity of Stotozhevoye, which had been fortified in the previous month. Half-buried T-34 tanks (with their turrets exposed) also took part in this bastion, along with the multi-calibre artillery, bunkers and thousands of mines that littered the bridgehead. In addition to the powerful T-34s, the mighty KV-1s also made their presence felt.

The fighting became fierce on the evening of that day, when a battle group from 30/I Battalion joined the attack. Again the Pz 38 tanks had to approach the T-34s to destroy them, as did the tank of Sergeant Csizmadia, who won the grand silver medal for valour that day. On the 10th a new effort was made to take Stotozhevoye, being the vanguard of the 30/3. In this battle several tanks, both Pz IV F-1 and Pz 38, were lost to the Soviet armoured tanks. Meanwhile, the right wing attacked in the direction of Uryv, capturing most of the city on the 10th. This victory was short-lived, however, as a Soviet counter-offensive managed to drive them out shortly afterwards.

▲ A damaged Toldi IIa shows its 40 mm cannon in the foreground. In particular, it bears the emblem adopted from 16 September 1942.

On the 11th, thanks to the efforts of the Hungarians and Germans, Stotozhevoye, completely destroyed, was finally conquered. Immediately, to take advantage of this blow to the Russians, armoured troops, including the 30th/2nd Battalion, were sent in the direction of the Ottitsiha Forest, where substantial Soviet troops were entrenched in favourable terrain. The Hungarians were severely punished by losing numerous armoured vehicles under heavy fire from the defenders, forcing them to redirect their attack to the south-east. The Soviets, noting the delicacy of the situation, sent the 54th and 130th Armoured Brigades, with numerous T-34s and KV-1s, to the bridgehead. These immediately proceeded to hit the attackers with heavy artillery fire from across the Don River, but without preventing the Soviets from retreating. The German troops of the 168th Infantry Division took advantage of this moment to take the new positions and entrench themselves in time to prepare for the new Soviet counter-offensive.

At dawn on the 12th, the T-34s and KV-1s demonstrated their superiority against the newly entrenched Germans, who were pushed back. The tanks of the 30/II Battalion led by Captain Kárpáthy came at them in another almost suicidal counterattack. The Soviet armoured vehicles, clearly superior to the Hungarian Pz 38 in terms of both armour and armament, destroyed a large number of them. Even the Pz IVs, which formed the core of the Hungarian armour, were unable to match the KV-1s and also fell under the blows of the Soviet armoured roller. Despite the carnage, however, the Hungarians, showing great courage, managed to repel the Soviet attack and recapture Stotozhevoye.

▲ The Toldi IIa was only a small improvement on the Toldi II, but it was still a long way from what the Magyar armoured force required.

By the end of the 12th, only 4 Pz IV and 22 Pz 38 were still in fighting condition; the next day they managed to destroy 8 T-34 armoured vehicles and damage 2 KV-1s in the new Soviet offensive. On the 14th the Soviets had still not managed to take Stotozhevoye, where the Hungarians and Germans were entrenched. Many of the Russian infantrymen were stopped by the Nimrod guns, whose zeroed cannons prevented the Russians from succeeding. Continuous fighting led to the 16th, when a new Soviet attack was stopped, resulting in the destruction of at least 24 tanks (including 6 KV-1s) by both Hungarian tanks and German anti-tank and assault guns. The third battle of Uryv ended on the same day, with a break for both sides.

The Hungarian 1st Armoured Division was left with only 2 Pz IV F-1 and 12 Pz-38 after the heavy fighting, suffering losses of 1237 killed and 6163 wounded. The overall result was that the bridgehead could not be eliminated and the losses were so heavy that the Hungarian armoured forces were left without combat capability. The 1st Armoured Division, cavalry squadrons and cyclist battalions had to be withdrawn from the front line to form reserve troops. Fortunately, there was a short respite for the Hungarians until January 1943 (interrupted only by a brief clash with Soviet armoured troops on 19 October), when they had to face a new Soviet offensive during the Ostrogozhsk-Rossosh operation.

The outcome of the fighting for the Hungarians was bittersweet, because although they had fought at a high level (like their Soviet opponents), the losses had been appalling. But where the Hungarians' clear inferiority was most evident was in their armaments, which had become completely obsolete and under-armed compared to their increasingly powerful Soviet rivals, such as the KV-1 and T-34.

This lack of power against enemy armour had not improved despite the use of the Toldi I or the Pz 38, and was only occasionally reversed with the arrival of the Pz IV. Faced with this alarming situation, the Hungarian government was forced to plan new armament strategies to improve Hungarian armoured capabilities in the near future. As a first emergency measure to compensate for the heavy Hungarian losses and to rebuild the 1st Armoured Division, the Germans agreed to give them, in October 1942, 10 Pz IV F-2, 10 Pz III M and perhaps between 4 and 8 Pz II F. In addition, in December, 10 German StuG III N with German crews were to be subordinated to the Hungarians.

As a curiosity, the Pz IIIs, which were integrated into the 30/5 armoured squadron, had to be manned by German personnel (about 50 men including officers, non-commissioned officers and soldiers of the 6th Panzer Regiment), while the Hungarians were trained, due to the lack of specialised personnel.

Regardless of the arrival of foreign material, Hungarian industries were already starting work on new vehicles that would be in front-line service within a few months, such as the Turán and Zrínyi, and that would increase Honved's potential.

On 3 October, army commander Gusztáv Jány complained to the Germans that he had not been supplied with the promised spare parts for his tanks. The Germans even pressurised the Hungarians to replace their commander, but the Hungarians refused.

The only significant Hungarian action took place on 19 October near Storozhevoye with part of Captain Mészöly's 30/I Tank Brigade destroying four Russian tanks.

At the end of November, the Red Army began its offensive against the southern flank of the Axis troops near Stalingrad, through the Italian and Romanian lines (remember that the Hungarian positions were a little further north). This attack forced the Germans to send reinforcements from other areas. The Hungarian rearguard troops were also moved, which considerably weakened the hold of their positions; a fact that would not go unnoticed by the Soviets, who would target the town of Uryv for a second large-scale winter offensive.

Opposite the Hungarian lines on the Don (which lay below the city of Voronezh), the troops of the Soviet Voronezh Front Army under the command of General Golikov were stationed. This initially consisted of the 40$^{th}$ Army (with eight rifle divisions, three tank brigades and three artillery divisions), the 18$^{th}$ Rifle Corps (with four rifle divisions and two tank brigades) and the 3$^{rd}$ Armoured Army (with eight rifle divisions, one rifle brigade, one cavalry corps, two tank corps and two artillery divisions).

Following the negative experiences the Hungarians had undergone on Soviet soil, where the extreme weakness of their armoured forces had become apparent, the High General Staff decided to implement the third part of the HUBA plan, HUBA III. This would be developed in the course of 1943 and, after numerous restructurings and the acquisition of more modern and effective equipment, would bring the Hungarian troops to a much higher level of combat capability, with the 2$^{nd}$ Army as the standard. Although this plan began to take shape during 1943, it would never be completed as originally planned due to the vicissitudes of war. Interestingly, from 1 December, the Infantry Brigade of the Armoured Division was renamed and organised as a motorised infantry regiment.

▲ In times of calm, the care and maintenance of the vehicle fleet was necessary, as in the case of this 38M Raba Botond.

▼ Impressive image of a Nimród in motion. Speed and high rate of fire were the strong points of these formidable vehicles.

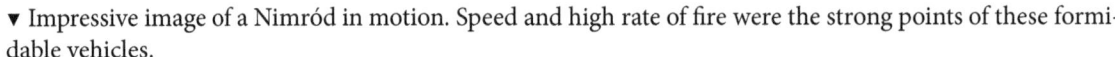

▲ Impressive view of the 40 mm cannon of the Nimród, which played an important role in Hungarian armoured units.

▲ Interesting aerial view of two Nimród self-propelled anti-aircraft guns during a military event in 1943, allowing a better view of their interior.

▼ Some Hungarian soldiers, well equipped against the cold, pose for the photographer in front of a Pz IV F1.

▲ Beautiful side view of a Nimród self-propelled anti-aircraft gun, one of the successes of the Hungarian armaments industry during the Second World War.

▼ The brand new Toldi II prototype poses for the camera with its camouflage silhouette clearly outlined.

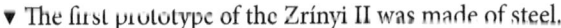

▲ One of the first Pz IV F2s in Hungarian hands. Compared to the F1 model, the firepower was greatly improved.

▼ The first prototype of the Zrínyi II was made of steel.

▲ Magyar troops during an engagement in their advance into the USSR in 1942.

▲ A 28M Pavesi carrying a 15 cm 31M howitzer in 1942.

▼ Axis offensive in the Soviet Union between 24 July and 18 November 1942. Public domain.

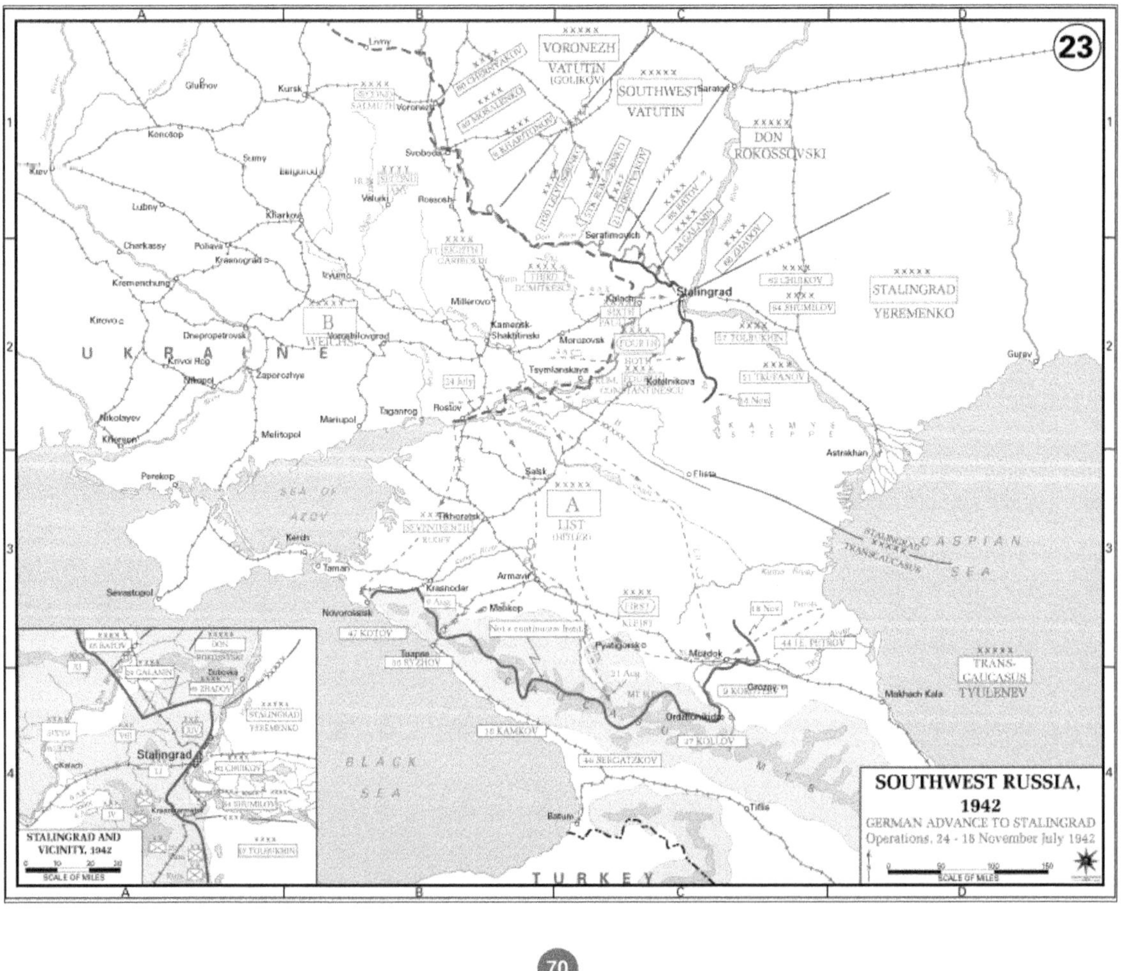

▲ Pz IV F1 manoeuvring down a slope. This tank was the first truly comparable to its rivals that the Magyar armoured weapon had at its disposal.

▼ A short-barreled Pz IV F1 prepares for future combat in the Esztergom-Szentistvánváros barracks in 1942. Until the arrival of the long-barreled Pz IV, this tank served its purpose well.

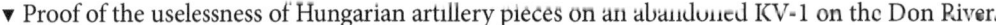

▲ A Hungarian soldier sits on a Toldi. On the turret of the tank both the Hungarian coat of arms, used for a time, which consists of a green cross with white borders on a red octagon, and the emblem of the mechanised troops are clearly visible.

▼ Proof of the uselessness of Hungarian artillery pieces on an abandoned KV-1 on the Don River.

# 1943: DISASTER AND REORGANISATION

## THE SOVIET ROLLER MAKES ITS APPEARANCE

The Hungarian troops deployed to the front began the year with very low temperatures but little activity at the front. On 2 January, the 1st Armoured Division was subordinated to Cramer Group (by its commander, Major General Hans Cramer), which in turn was the only reserve unit of Army Group B. Cramer Group consisted of the German 26th and 168th Divisions, the German 26th and 168th Divisions, the German 1st Armoured Detachment and the German 1st Armoured Detachment. The Cramer Group consisted of the German 26th and 168th Divisions, the 190th Assault Cannon Detachment and the German 700th Armoured Detachment.

▲ One of the few Marder IIs that served Hungary. Its formidable firepower represented a major improvement for the Hungarian armoured forces.

▲ The complete equipment of a Bofors anti-aircraft artillery piece in 1943.

▲ Two soldiers posing next to a Hansa Lloyd 37M half-track, normally used as a tractor for artillery pieces.

On 6 January, the Hungarians received five Marder II destroyers on loan (under the command of Captain Zergényi), which were to be manned by Hungarians from the 51st anti-aircraft self-propelled battalion and the 30th armoured regiment. In order for the new crews to get up to speed, four German instructors were stationed with them at Puskino. These destroyers were integrated into a new unit called the 1st Independent Destroyer Company, which contributed its powerful 75 mm guns to the depleted Hungarian armoured arsenal. On 7 January, the Hungarians had 16 Pz IV (8 short-barreled and 8 long-barreled), 41 Pz 38, two 38M Toldi Is, 5 Marder, some 40M Nimrod and 9 Pz III Ms.
But this calm situation was about to change, for on 12 January 1943 there was a powerful Soviet attack against the front line held by the Hungarian troops (deployed to protect the northern flank of the Italian VIIIth Army separating them from the Romanian troops with the IVth Army), which, as already mentioned, the Soviets knew to be rather weak in terms of troops (on 1 January the IInd Army did not reach 195,000 men). The result was a disaster, as the exhausted Magyar troops were waiting to be replaced by fresh troops, which had not yet been deployed at the time of the attack.

▲ An anti-aircraft fire exercise with two Nimród and one Bofors cannon, all 40 mm.

▼ The Marder was based on the Pz II chassis (in various models such as the A/B/C/F). With its powerful 75 mm cannon and despite the few units supplied to Hungary on loan, it became one of the best weapons available to the Hungarians against Soviet armoured.

The attack was conducted from three different zones in an attempt to collapse the Axis defences. The three drop zones were Uryv, Schutschye and Kantemirovka, where the Soviets had large contingents ready. The weather was extreme, with a thick blanket of snow and temperatures hovering around 30 degrees Celsius at night and 20 degrees Celsius during the day.

From the Uryv bridgehead, Moskalenko's Soviet 40th Army attacked with one Guard Rifle Division, four Rifle Divisions, one Rifle Brigade, three Tank Brigades with 164 tanks, including 33 KV-1s and 58 T-34s, as well as other artillery, tank destroyers, rocket launchers, etc. From its positions and after overtaking the Magyars, it was planned to link up with Rybalko's 3rd Armoured Army. Further north of the Magyars, Chernyakhovsky's 60th Army and Chibisov's 38th Army were to keep the German 2nd Army occupied.

From the Schutschye bridgehead, the Soviet 18th Army Corps attacked with three rifle divisions, a rifle brigade, two tank brigades with 99-150 tanks, including 1 KV-1 and 56 T-34s, and various artillery elements.

From the Kantemirovka area the Soviet 3rd Armoured Army with 425 tanks, including 29 KV-1 and 221 T-34.

▲ Hungarian Marder IIs bore the original German emblem. Here is one of these destroyer tanks in action at the front.

▲ Another image of a Hungarian Marder used during the retreat ceremony of the Hungarian 2nd Army.

The 40th Army attacked in two directions: towards Alekseyevka (where it converged with the 3rd Armoured Army from the south) and also towards Ostrogosshk (where it converged with the 18th Rifle Corps). The Soviet artillery preparation was very powerful from all three attack drop zones. The offensive was initially planned to be launched on 14 January from the three target areas, but the actual start was a large reconnaissance attack from the Uryv bridgehead on 12 January on the weakest part of the Hungarian defence (where the 4th Infantry Regiment of the 7th Light Division was located). On the same day, after an intense artillery attack, six reinforced Soviet battalions supported by tanks attacked the positions of the 4th/IIIth Battalion causing heavy losses to the Hungarians and managing to break through and advance three kilometres westwards. On the morning of 13 January, a Hungarian counterattack, supported by the Germans, was unsuccessful. The German 700th Armoured Detachment, close to the Uryv bridgehead and equipped with obsolete Pz 38s, was practically annihilated by the Soviet 150th Armoured Brigade. On the 14th, the Soviet 18th Rifle Corps attacked and penetrated the Hungarian defensive line of the 12th Light Division near Schutschye. The Hungarians with their artillery pieces managed to destroy at least nine Soviet tanks, but Hungarian weakness eventually forced them to retreat. On 14 January from Kantemirovka the Soviet 3rd Armoured Army broke through the defensive lines.

▲ Several Hungarian tanks, including two Pz IIs in the foreground, lie in a depot, perhaps waiting to be overhauled for deployment as soon as possible.

Until the evening of 15 January, the armoured troops attacking from Uryv were hard hit, mostly by infantrymen attacking the steel giants with mines or any available weapon. The 116th Armoured Brigade lost 31 of 47 tanks (including 15 KV-1s), the 150th Armoured Brigade was virtually destroyed with only 4 of 43 tanks remaining, the 86th Armoured Brigade lost 7 tanks and the 150th Armoured Brigade had to be withdrawn from the offensive. The courage of the Hungarian troops was more than evident, as shown by Corporal Pandur who destroyed 3 tanks with anti-tank mines during the January fighting.

▲ The commander of the Toldi I poses for the camera. The octagonal tricolour emblem and the white eagle of an armoured cavalry battalion are clearly visible on both the door and the side of the vehicle.

▲ A Toldi I, recognisable by its antenna, takes part in a parade after the first Hungarian border battles.

▼ The commander of a Toldi II poses for the camera. One can see the octagonal tricolour emblem and to his right the coat of arms of the mechanised section of the Hungarian army.

The confusion was total, as many units lacked even the proper armament and ammunition, so all the veteran Hungarian troops could do was try to resist the hell that was breaking loose in front of them in a line between Mitrofanovka and Kantemirovka and only retreat in the most orderly manner possible when they ran the risk of being overwhelmed by the Soviets (as indeed happened with the 7th and 12th Divisions) with the consequent risk of being surrounded. For their part, the men who had just arrived at the front did not know how to react adequately to the Soviet horde, and panic quickly spread through their ranks, causing the already shaky front line to disband and collapse. Perhaps the only support that could have attempted to stabilise the front, the 1st Hungarian Armoured Division, was not initially sent to support its compatriots because it was subordinate to German troops and was not given permission to do so (perhaps due to German indecision in the face of the speed of events). To complicate matters further, on the 14th, the southernmost defensive line of the Magyar (held by the Italians) was also broken through by another powerful Soviet attack.

The Hungarian 1st Armoured Division's counter-attack finally took place on 16 January, after they were ordered to try to seal the remaining gaps in the defensive line from Woytsche, which had been captured by Soviet troops. Despite their efforts, it was too late to have any significant effect against the Soviet assault and they had to withdraw shortly afterwards, after a counter order, because they risked being surrounded by the enemy. On the 16th, from the Uryv bridgehead, the Soviets had penetrated an area 45 km wide and 60 km deep, from Schutschye into an area 50 km wide and 35 km deep and from Kantemirovka into an area 30 km wide and 90 km deep, inside the German-Hungarian lines.

▲ Picture of a T-34/75 captured by the Hungarians with the national colours (red, white and green) painted on the turret. Only on very rare occasions were they used in combat against their original owners.

Faced with such a defeat, with very low temperatures and a thick layer of snow, the Hungarian armoured troops received a new order to support and cover the retreat of the Hungarian troops as much as possible, as well as to hold the towns of Nicolayevka and Alekseyevka, vital for the escape route.

On 17 January, Soviet troops seized the town of Alekseyevka with the cooperation of the partisans. The Hungarian troops were not sufficient to protect it, leaving only the town of Ilovskoye (north of Alekseyevka) under Magyar control. On the evening of the 17th, the Hungarian Armoured Division carried out a counter-attack with 8 PZ III and 4 PZ IV in the direction of Dolschik-Ostrogosshk, destroying a column of Soviet vehicles. On Cramer's orders, they had to retreat, leaving behind a PZ IV after a rupture that immobilised it. On that day, the Division lost a lot of equipment that had to be left behind and blown up due to lack of fuel and various ruptures in the vehicles. The Pz 38s were totally useless in the deep snow and extreme temperatures; the 30/I Battalion had to fly at least 17 Pz 38s, 2 Pz IVs and other vehicles because they could not take them with them on the retreat.

▲ Several French-made Hotchkiss H-39 tanks were placed next to anti-aircraft in second-line positions. All these vehicles were lost in the course of anti-partisan operations.

On 18 January, the Armoured Division's mission was to attack and recapture Alekseyevka with the support of the subordinate German 559th Tank Detachment. In this attack, a Hungarian Pz III was blown up by a mine and at least four enemy tanks were destroyed. After two and a half hours of fighting and thanks to the courage with which the Magyars behaved in such a critical situation, the town was recaptured. The losses were, in addition to the aforementioned PZ III, two Pz IVs destroyed by anti-tank pieces and a Nimród of the 51/2 Squadron by a mine. The leader of 30/3 Platoon, Sergeant Bovojcsov, was killed in this attack. After the capture of the city, the commander of 30/5 Armoured Squadron, Lieutenant Dalitz, lost his life: he did not pay sufficient attention when his Pz III passed over the frozen Tiayazosna River and the ice cracked, sinking his tank (only one crew member was saved). Subsequent fighting led to the destruction of a single T-60 in the northern sector of the city by a Marder II, which together with the Engineer Company of the 30th Armoured Regiment and an artillery battery managed to seal off the Stojanow-Dalnij road.

▲Magyar soldiers train in their training camp in 1943. These soldiers fought with all their might until the end of the world conflict, when Hungary was conquered by the Soviets.

On the morning of 19 January, the Soviets attacked from the south, a Pz IV destroyed a T-60, while a T-34 was destroyed south-west of the city by a Marder II. The relentless Soviet advance, despite heavy losses, drove the Hungarians to retreat from the city, unable to hold it. During the retreat, two Nimród of the 51/1 Squadron were destroyed by Soviet anti-tank guns. On 18 and 19 January, many retreating troops managed to escape a possible encirclement of Alekseyevaka, including the Armoured Division. On 20 January, a Pz IV was lost when it was captured by Soviet soldiers disguised as Germans who tricked its men. During the night of 20-21 January, a Division battle group destroyed the railway line and part of the Alekseyevka railway station. On 21 January, the Hungarian Armoured Division began a counter-attack to assist the retreat of the German 23rd Infantry Division, behind which came the troops that had defended Ostrogosshk until 19 January, when they had to withdraw due to lack of ammunition (the Hungarian 13th Light Division and the German 168th Infantry Division). The last Hungarian troops to withdraw from Ostrogosshk actually did so at dawn on 20 January. A new Hungarian counterattack succeeded in destroying a Soviet reconnaissance group and retaking the western part of Alekseyevka, holding it until the night of the 20th, with some Soviet counterattacks repulsed. A Marder II from the 559th German Tank Detachment destroyed a Soviet armoured reconnaissance vehicle. Throughout the night and day of 22 January, the Soviets continued their attacks, while the Hungarians

▲ The crew of a Zrínyi II poses for the camera through the hatches in a photograph taken at a training camp around March 1944.

▲ A Turán I during manoeuvres to ascend a dike.

▲ Several Turán IIs ready to be transported by train to the USSR after their capture.

held their positions. In the morning of that day, a Hungarian Marder II destroyed a T-34 and a T-60. On 23 January, the Division began to withdraw from Ilynka, acting as a rear guard for Kramer Group, reaching Noviy Oskol on 25 January.

In only eight days from the start of the offensive, the Soviets managed to eliminate the last defensive enclaves of the exhausted Hungarian forces in villages such as Novo Charkovka, Novo Postoialovka, Kopani, Valuiki and Podgornoye, from which only a few thousand men managed to escape. By 27 January, the Hungarian 2nd Army was largely annihilated.

After a few days of calm and quiet, Soviet troops began a powerful attack on Noviy Oskol at dawn on 28 January. There, in the north-eastern suburb, was the 30/6th Armoured Squadron, which lost its leader, First Lieutenant Balázs, with his Pz IV. In this attack there were multiple clashes in the streets of the city. Tank platoon commander Miklos Jonas distinguished himself in the fighting during those days, for which he was awarded the Gold Medal for Valour for his courageous behaviour (he was the only tank commander to receive this award during the Second World War).

Finally, the Magyar Armoured Division left the city and retreated towards Mikhaylowka, a village east of Korotscha. On this 28th day, the Division lost 26 men (mostly wounded), apart from Pz IV, which was left behind. The next two days were quieter, but on 31 January, a new Soviet attack was launched against the Division's positions. These were repulsed by two counter-attacks on 1 and 3 February. On the 3rd, after heavy fighting, they succeeded in repelling a Soviet battalion that had briefly cut off men from the Grossdeutschland, the 168th German Infantry Division and the Hungarian Armoured Division. On 4 February, the Armoured Division again repulsed the Soviet attacks and was finally ordered to retreat in the direction of Korotscha in the face of enormous pressure from the adversaries. There the Division was subordinated to the German 168th Infantry Division under Lieutenant General Kraiss. On the morning of 6 February, the Hungarian Division managed to repel several Soviet counter-attacks after heavy fighting. On the morning of 7 February, Korotscha was surrounded on three of its flanks and a new Soviet attack was launched at 4.45 am. The last two remaining Nimród in the Division fired into the darkness with zero elevation of their guns, successfully stopping the Soviet counter-attack. Another attack by over 500 Soviet troops was repulsed by the Nimrods in a final effort shortly afterwards. After all other units had withdrawn from Korotscha, it was the turn of the Armoured Division, still fighting. The two Nimród had to be blown up by the Hungarians themselves due to the impossibility of rescuing and towing them after they were trapped in the terrain. In this attack, the last Pz 38 of the Division was also lost to enemy anti-tank fire. The last serious fighting took place on 7 February; on 9 February, the Armoured Division crossed the Donetz River, reached Charkow and finally withdrew from the front line. At this point, the Hungarian unit's only remaining armoured vehicles were two Marders, which were sent back to Germany in the summer of 1943 at the end of their lease period.

Parallel to the vicissitudes of the Armoured Division, it must be remembered that the Hungarian III Corps had its own hell; after the attacks of 14 January, it was isolated in the north. It had to be subordinated to the German II Corps, which used it as 'cannon fodder'. Within

III Corps, the 9th Light Division remained on the banks of the Don until 29 January, as on 28 January Kastornoye (where the Hungarian infantrymen were deployed) was almost completely encircled by the Soviet 13th and 40th Armies, forcing them to abandon their positions. The risk of being encircled was further increased by the fact that the Hungarians were forbidden by the Germans to use the evacuation roads, which the Germans used to retreat. The Hungarians therefore had to march through thick snow and without the proper equipment. The behaviour of the Germans and in particular of the commander-in-chief of the 2nd Army, Lieutenant General Siebert, provoked a great feeling of hatred towards the Germans in most of the survivors of the 3rd Hungarian Corps.

▲ Several trucks used by Hungarian troops in a barracks in Honvéd in 1943. Various models of different origins can be seen, such as the Ford or the German Hanomag.

1943 had started disastrously for the Magyars, who lost most of their troops and armaments during the Soviet offensive, estimated at about half of the total available equipment of the entire Hungarian army. The losses after all these fights were 107 tanks (22 Pz IV, 10 Pz III, 64 Pz 38, 11 Toldi), 3 Marder II, 15 Nimród, 10 Csaba, 1030 motor vehicles (681 trucks, 114 cars, 235 motorbikes), 17 10.5 cm artillery guns, 20 anti-tank guns, 8 anti-aircraft guns, as well as a multitude of minor weapons. Nevertheless, the conduct of the Hungarian soldiers led to more than 3,000 German and Hungarian decorations during the fierce fighting in which they participated between 1942 and 1943.

## ARMOURED FORMATIONS IN THE OCCUPATION TROOPS

One must not forget the Hungarian troops that were in the rear and carried out occupation duties, as they too had their own armoured fleet. In January 1942, the Hungarian occupation command was organised into five infantry brigades, two cyclist battalions (II and VII) and other support troops, to which were added two tank formations formed in 1942: the 101st and 102nd Independent Tank Squadron (the 103rd cannot be confirmed as existing according to current reports), which participated in the support of Hungarian anti-partisan activities on Ukrainian territory. The 101st received French tanks from the spoils of war captured in France from the Germans: two Somua S-35s that served as command vehicles and 15 Hotchkiss H-35/H-39s, while the 102nd used Hungarian-made vehicles. The Magyars also had three Renault R-35s, which were mainly used as tractors due to their low military value.

The independent 101st Squadron was organised as the 1st Tank Battalion in October 1942, with Major Pongrácz as commander. In its combat order it had one heavy platoon and three light platoons. The heavy platoon included two S-35s, while the light platoons had 15 H-35/H-39s. The missions of these units were the usual ones for rearguard troops in enemy territory, such as escorting convoys, clearing roads, capturing partisans, and were sometimes used for occasional attacks. The tanks were usually transported by train across the vast Ukrainian countryside, allowing them to reach the area of interest faster than they would have done by their own means, while reducing wear and tear on the tanks. All these French tanks were gradually lost in the period 1942-1944 for various reasons: attacks by partisans or regular Soviet troops, and in some cases destroyed by their own crews because they could not retreat with them, thus preventing them from falling intact into enemy hands.

The 102nd was organised as the 1/II Tank Battalion in 1943, with two light tank platoons with 3 Toldi each and two armoured vehicle platoons with 3 Csaba each. It was commanded by Major Parázsó and was tasked to serve as a small reserve force for the occupation troops. In December 1943 it was located in Kremenyec and later moved to Stanislau. The 102nd was disbanded after the arrival of the 2nd Armoured Division in Galicia in April 1944.

Among the occupation forces, the Hungarians also used two captured armoured trains, one from the Poles and one from the Soviets. Thanks to them, they had important mobile artillery support against partisan units in their numerous movements through the occupied areas.

The last remaining armoured contingent to be mentioned is that of the eight 39M Csaba, which made up the 7th Cyclist Battalion's armoured company, engaged in support and reconnaissance missions.

## DISENGAGE FROM GERMANY, BUT HOW?

As we have seen in these lines, the cream of the Hungarian fighting force, the 2ª Hungarian Army, despite its enormous individual displays of courage and daring, had lost 70-80% of its strength, with a significant number of dead, wounded and captured (50,000, 50,000 and 28,000 respectively). By March, the 1st Armoured Division, already withdrawn from the front line, had only about 8,000 men, 500 vehicles and 13 guns. This severe attrition of the Hungarian formation became evident when on 24 May 1943 only about 40,000 men and a small part of their original armoured equipment managed to return to Hungary after the German High Command allowed this withdrawal (due to the complete unusability of their shattered remains).

After the events on the Russian front, the Hungarian government realised that Hungary could not stand by Germany in this conflict, as it would be impossible to do so materially without leading the country to annihilation. But Germany, which knew what the Hungarians were thinking, could not allow this. Moreover, it demanded the deployment of new Hungarian troops both in the USSR and in the Balkans. While trying to reorganise his forces, Horthy, in order to satisfy German wishes, sent two army corps (the 6th to the Ukraine and the 8th to Belarus) to the Eastern Front for rearguard tasks against the numerous and powerful Soviet partisan parties in the occupied territories. On this occasion, the armoured forces were minimal. Due to the large area to be covered (approximately 100 by 450 kilometres), it was decided that it would be more effective to divide into small units and garrisons. During this task, the Magyars did their best, bearing in mind that the shortage of men and the obsolete armament they carried limited their actions. Nevertheless, they managed to eliminate many of the partisan strongpoints in the area.

Faced with incessant demands for troops from the Germans, Hungary could only delay the deployment of these new troops while they began to establish contacts with the Allies for a separate peace. The Hungarians tried to make small movements of their soldiers that would make the Allies realise their willingness to get closer to them, such as General Szombathelyi's request to Germany to withdraw its occupation troops to Soviet territory, under the pretext of strengthening its borders in the face of Soviet advances, which in some areas were just over a hundred kilometres from the Carpathians. The Germans obviously watched any Hungarian activity carefully, especially after Italy's defection in September 1943.

These secret contacts were made known in the London press, when it was reported that meetings for this purpose had taken place on 1 and 2 June 1943. Evidently, when the Germans became aware of this news, they began to tighten their control over any Hungarian political movements. But the negotiations were not successful, as the Allies demanded that Hungary declare war on Germany if it accepted such a peace. Thus Hungary found itself caught between two equally terrible escapes.

In the reorganisation of the Hungarian Army, infantry divisions were to be transformed into combined divisions and rearguards, the decimated 1st Armoured Division was to be rebuilt after its destruction on the Eastern Front and a new armoured formation, the 2nd Armoured Division, was to be created. New units such as the 1st Hussar Cavalry Division or the "Szent Laszlo" Parachute Division or the 1st Assault Tank Battalion (assault artillery) were also to be created.

As for the assault artillery, it should be noted that the first men to join the course for these units did so between 18 July and 31 August 1943, under the command of Captain József Barankay, who had attended a German assault artillery course in Jüteborg (Germany). The base of the 1st Assault Tank Battalion was established on 1 September in Hajmáskér (the main Hungarian military training camp) with only three Zrínyi, and on 1 October both the 1st Assault Tank Battalion and the 2nd-8th Assault Tank Training Group were fully available for training. By the beginning of August 1943, 1925 men (including 113 officers) had been drafted into the new assault tank unit. The lack of Zrinyi forced the use of the Toldi and Turan while awaiting their arrival (before 1 September, they had trained with two Turan and the steel prototype Zrinyi, so with more Turan available and the Zrinyi based on them, it was logical to use them). Both the Toldi and the Turan were mainly used for communications, guidance and other technical training, but fire training was only conducted with the Turan's short 75 mm cannons, due to their similarity to the Zrinyi, compared to the cannons of the Toldi.

# ANNEX

## INSIGNIA OF THE HUNGARIAN ARMOURED FORCES

The insignia used by the Magyar armoured forces varied during the course of the conflict. In fact, at least nine different models were used between 1938 and 1945. In these lines, we will briefly look at the most commonly used ones.

The first insignia used by the Magyar armoured forces was the triangular tricolour (red, white and green) already in use in the Hungarian Air Force. This insignia was used on an armoured train, specifically the 102nd Armoured Train, during the Slovak campaign in 1938. To overcome the lack of a common national insignia for armoured troops, it was decided in July 1940 to hold a competition in which the various units would propose an insignia to be chosen for use by all units. The first widespread insignia consisted of a Maltese Cross with different colours on the border and a circle on the inside that also varied in colour from unit to unit. This insignia was painted on all vehicles participating in military operations in Transylvania, Yugoslavia and later Ukraine.

▲ The coat of arms of the Maltese Cross is visible on this tank of Csaba's, which places the photo just before the Second World War.

Despite its use, however, the Maltese Cross insignia did not convince the Magyars in high places, who decided to adopt another design with a cross similar to the one used on German vehicles (which would have made it easier to recognise each other on the front line), but with some peculiarities. The insignia consisted of a green cross with white borders on a red hexagonal background and came into service immediately after the Hungarian occupation of the Yugoslav territories in the spring of 1941. As can be seen, its use partly coincides with that of the Maltese Cross, which is quite true, since many units were equipped with the new insignia while others still wore the old one. This insignia was intended to become the unified emblem of the Magyar armoured forces. According to the original order, the insignia was to be painted on both sides and on the roof of the turrets, as well as on the front and rear of the vehicle. The width of the insignia varied according to the size of the armoured vehicle, with a width of 350 mm for smaller armoured vehicles and 500 mm for larger ones.

▲ A fully crewed Nimród during manoeuvres.

Not long after its introduction, voices began to be heard disagreeing with the insignia. These came mainly from the crews (and more precisely the pilots) of the Csaba Toldi or Nimród who were already wearing them. The reason for their complaints was that the size, brightness and contrast of the insignia gave the crews the feeling of being right behind a target. This fact, together with the limited war potential of the Hungarian armour, obviously did not help the morale of the crews at all. It was this discomfort, along with other causes, that prompted the Magyar military high command to decide to change the insignia to more suitable ones.

Thus, on 16 November 1942, the order was issued to replace the previous tricolour insignia with a new one to be used by all vehicles of the Hungarian armoured forces. This new unifying insignia was nothing more than a copy of the one used by the Hungarian air force and consisted of a white cross on a black square.

This new insignia had to be painted on the sides of the vehicle and on the surface of the engines in a variable size depending on the size of the vehicle (there were three predefined sizes for this situation). As a curiosity, it was not required on the sides of the turrets of armoured vehicles; but it was tacitly (unofficially) forbidden to wear it on the front of vehicles, because it was again considered a target for the driver's seat. This insignia was used until the

▲ Side view of a Zrínyi II in which one can clearly see the emblem with the white cross on a black square that the Magyar armoured troops wore for much of the war.

end of the war, co-existing with the German insignia discussed below.

After the arrival of numerous armoured vehicles from the German Reich in 1944, in many cases they retained both the original paintwork brought from Germany and the German insignia. It is true that two reasons may have influenced this:
- On the one hand, Magyar troops began to be fully integrated into German units, so it was reasonable that, to avoid any misunderstanding, the German insignia should be respected.
- On the other hand, the urgent need to put the vehicles from Germany into service made the 'fun' of painting the Hungarian insignia on them virtually impossible. They were only painted with the corresponding tactical numbering and so went into battle.

▲ The only existing photograph of the prototype 15 cm Nebelwerfer rocket launcher on a Zrínyi II. Had it been mass-produced, the Hungarian army would have acquired the necessary firepower that it lacked for the duration of the war.

▲ The only example of the Toldi PaK 40 L/48 destroyer. Its numerous disadvantages in mass production led to its abandonment.

▼ Disassembled prototype of the Turán III tank turret.

# BIBLIOGRAPHY

Unknown, *The Royal Hungarian gendarmerie and police during world war II.*

Axworthy, Mark. *Third Axis Fourth Ally.* Arms and Armour. 1995.

Baczoni, Tamás; Tóth, László. *Hungarian Army Uniforms. 1939-1945.* Huniform Books. 2010.

Barnaky, Péter. *Panther on the battlefield.* Volume 6. PeKo Publishing. 2014.

Becze, Csaba. *Magyar Steel.* Stratus. 2006.

Bernád, Denes; Kliment, Charles K. *Magyar warriors. The history of the Royal Hungarian Armed Forces 1919-1945.* Volume I. Helion & Company. 2015.

Bernád, Denes; Kliment, Charles K. *Magyar warriors. The history of the Royal Hungarian Armed Forces 1919-1945.* Volume II. Helion & Company. 2017.

Bonhardt, Attila. *Zrínyi II assault howitzer.* PeKo Publishing. 2015.

Caballero, C; Molina, L. *Panzer IV. El puño de la Wehrmacht.* AF Editores. 2006.

Gladysiak, L; Karmieh, S. *Panzer IV Ausf. H and Ausf.J.* Vol I. Kagero 2015.

Gladysiak, L; Karmieh, S. *Panzer IV Ausf. H and Ausf.J.* Vol II. Kagero 2016.

Guillemot, Philippe. *Hungary 1944-45. The panzers' last stand.* Histoire&Collections. 2010.

Kerekes András. *The role and creation of the Royal Hungarian assault artillery, and the Zrínyi II assault howitzers.* Hadmérnök. X Évfolyam 2 szám. 2015 június.

Magyaródy, SJ. *Hungary and the Hungarians.* Matthias Corvinus Publishers.

Mc Taggart, Patrick. *¡Asedio!.* Inédita Editores SL. 2010.

Mujzer, Peter. *Huns on wheels.* Mujzer&Partner Ltd.

Oliver, Dennis. *Tiger I and Tiger II tanks.* Germany army and Waffen-SS Eastern Front 1944. Pen & Sword Military. 2016.

Order of battle and handbook of the Hungarian armed forces. February 1944. USA War department.

Restayn, Jean. *Tiger I in action 1942-1945.* Histoire & Collections.2013.

Thomas, Nigel; Pál Szábo, László. *The Royal Hungarian Army in World War II.* Osprey Publishing. 2008.

Tirone, Laurent. Panzer. *The German tanks encyclopedia.* Caraktere. 2016.

Ungváry, Krisztián. *Battle for Budapest.100 days in World War II.* IB Tauris. 2003.

Ungváry, Krisztián. *The "Second Stalingrad": The destruction of Axis forces at Budapest (february 1945).* Hungarian Studies Review, Vol XXII, nº 1 (Spring, 1995).

Wood, Ian Michael. *History of the Totenkopf's Panther-Abteilung.* PeKo Publishing. 2015.

Zaloga, Steven J. *Tanks of Hitler´seastern allies. 1941-45.* Osprey Publishing. 2013.

# TITOLI GIÀ PUBBLICATI - TITLES ALREADY PUBLISHING

www.ingramcontent.com/pod-product-compliance
Lightning Source LLC
LaVergne TN
LVHW072118060526
838201LV00068B/4918